Rev. Phil

Y0-BNF-457

# BETHLEHEM LUTHERAN LIBRARY

A15
FER

Thompson, Mervin E.
Starting Over Single

# Starting Over SINGLE

# Starting Over Single

## MERVIN E. THOMPSON

**PRINCE OF PEACE PUBLISHING**
Burnsville, Minnesota 55337

STARTING OVER SINGLE
Copyright © 1985 Prince of Peace Publishing, Inc.

All rights reserved. No portion of this book may be reproduced in any form, except for brief quotations in reviews, without the written permission of the publishers.

Unless otherwise indicated, Scripture quotations are from the Revised Standard Version of the Bible (RSV), copyrighted 1946, 1952, © 1971, 1973 by the Division of Christian Education of the National Council of Churches of Christ in the U.S.A., are used by permission.

Library of Congress Catalog Card Number
Thompson, Mervin E.,1941
    Starting Over Single

Bibliography: p.
1. Single People—Religious Life  2. Divorce People—  3. Divorce Biblical—
4. Teaching. I. Title.
BV4596.S5T47       1985       248.4'8413104       85-3638
ISBN 0-933173-00-8

*Printed in the United States of America*

*In* Gratitude
*to my wife Jackie
and children Deanna & Noel*
*for all of their wonderful
love & support*

# CONTENTS

ACKNOWLEDGEMENTS / 9

INTRODUCTION / 11

CHAPTER ONE
DIVORCE / 15

CHAPTER TWO
DIVORCE IS A DEATH / 26

CHAPTER THREE
AN UNDERSTANDING OF GOD / 34

CHAPTER FOUR
THE OLD TESTAMENT AND DIVORCE / 43

CHAPTER FIVE
THE NEW TESTAMENT AND DIVORCE / 56

CHAPTER SIX
UNDER THE INFLUENCE OF CHEMICALS / 68

CHAPTER SEVEN
BRINGING MYSELF INTO FOCUS / 82

CHAPTER EIGHT
CHILDREN OF DIVORCE / 103

CHAPTER NINE
RELATIONSHIPS: OLD AND NEW / 112

CHAPTER TEN
TWELVE STEPS FOR SPIRITUAL GROWTH AND RENEWAL / 126

CHAPTER ELEVEN
STARTING OVER SINGLE / 138

APPENDIX
HOW TO MAKE AN SOS COURSE WORK / 144

BIBLIOGRAPHY / 158

# ACKNOWLEDGMENTS

I am deeply indebted to the people of Prince of Peace Lutheran Church in Burnsville, Minnesota, for the opportunity they have given to me to minister to them and to do some writing. Special thanks must go to the congregational leaders during the time of the creation of this book, Jack Fenton, Gail Steel and Lois Helvick.

Prince of Peace is a congregation of the American Lutheran Church, and is located just south of Minneapolis at a place called the Ridges. The Ridges is a 140 acre site owned by Fairview Community Hospitals. In 1985 it contains a full service hospital, a nursing home and three medical clinics. Within five years new construction will include housing for the elderly, some residential housing, a YMCA and more medical office space. Prince of Peace is located right in the middle of the Ridges and serves as the spiritual center. We think it is a magnificent place to be.

Much credit for the planning and implementation of our Starting Over Single program should go to Dee Hehir, Barb Bishop, Norlyn Smith and Jerry Jorgensen. We will never forget our first trembling efforts of putting together a program and a brochure, wondering if anyone would attend. We planned for 25 at the first seminar and 110 people showed up. We knew then we were meeting a crisis need.

Several people have given me much input and feedback to the written material in the book. Bonnie Wedger, Mike Oiseth, Maryalys Morphew, Karen Halvorson and Dee Hehir were most helpful in suggesting priorities and directions. Wayne Skaff, who serves as director of administration of Prince of Peace and is the driving force in our publishing company, has given invaluable help. Mary Jeanne Benson has been an outstanding secretary and proof reader. I am very grateful to all of these people.

I am also indebted to the speakers at our seminars who have contributed so much to this book. Rev. Ted Kalkwarf is the Counseling Pastor at Prince of Peace. Rev. Janet Tidemann is the Associate Pastor of St. James Lutheran Church in Burnsville. Dr. Vern Bittner is the Executive Director for the Institute for Christian Living. Dee Hehir is a member of Prince of Peace and a leader in our singles ministry. Thanks again to these tremendous communicators.

A final word of gratitude must go to Dr. Kenneth Chafin, pastor of South Main Baptist Church in Houston, Texas. I was fortunate enough to attend the Billy Graham School of Evangelism some years ago when Dr. Chafin described the ministry to singles in his own congregation and gave special emphasis to a four-week course entitled "Beginning Again". We took that original idea and then built on it. I am very thankful to Dr. Chafin for his inspiration and encouragement.

# INTRODUCTION

Our family moved to Burnsville, Minnesota, a community just south of Minneapolis, in 1970. It was a very young suburban community at the time, with a few housing developments, a smattering of stores and churches and schools, and little else. Most of the residents lived in single family homes, a few apartment buildings were also present. A common stereotype was that each family had 2.2 children, the oldest nearing junior high age. Most of the men worked in some educational field or the computer industry, while the majority of the women were homemakers. There was a strong homogeneity, of background, of experience, of family makeup.

It was not difficult for churches to program for such families, those people who have been referred to as YUMPies (Young Upwardly Mobile Professionals). The primary task of the church was to have sufficient room and volunteers for Sunday School and confirmation, to have a very active program and a large nursery. The main pressures in life as the Vietnam War gasped its final breath and Richard Nixon fought for his political life had to do with climbing the corporate ladder and enduring the politics of the local athletic organizations. This was a bedroom community made up of a strong religious component, with about one third of the people being Catholic, one third Lutheran, and one third other or no religious background.

We were not exactly sleeping through the revolution, but looking back it is amazing how quickly everything changed. By the mid-70's we began to notice that the stereotype mentioned above was no longer valid. The role of women was changing. Condominiums and townhouses were springing up all around us. The family was under attack from many quarters, and the word "divorce" crept slowly and surely into our vocabulary.

At times we felt almost under siege. Day after day and week after week came new reports of families going under. We began to ask ourselves "Which family will be next? Isn't there anything we can do? We don't believe in divorce, what should be the church's response?" We tried to slap band-aids on open wounds, but that sometimes did more harm than good. Meanwhile, we noticed a dramatic rise in single persons in our community, divorced, widowed, never married. Churches did not know what to do.

A turning point for me came in the late 1970's when a group of our singles decided that I needed some remedial education about the world of singles. They presented me with a book entitled *Saturday Night, Sunday Morning*, written by Nicholas Christoff. This book showed me how out of touch we had been with the single population. It also warned that if the church was to begin to reach single people with any degree of effectiveness, we would have to make some significant changes. Without change, the church simply would not appeal to singles.

This realization was rather disturbing to us at Prince of Peace, for congregations usually do not want to change. We would rather stay the way we are, and insist that others do the changing. But we decided to bite the bullet and attempted to make some important changes. We very intentionally began to change our language, the words we used about women and men and marriage and families and singles. We said for the first time that it is okay to be single, one does not have to be married to be a complete person.

We also changed our attitude toward divorce. This was not easy. When people are afraid of something they often tend to react with hostility toward those who remind them of this fear. But we attempted to recognize that divorce was really a death in the family, a death in the church, and that those in the midst of it needed all of the love and support and prayers that would be required in any other experience of death.

We also changed our programming. One of these new programs was our Starting Over Single seminars. In a way this has been at the heart of our commitment to change and our commitment to a singles ministry.

It has not been hard to see some of the results. Sunday mornings find large numbers of single persons in worship, often sitting together as an extended family. Our new member classes are often filled with single persons, the majority of them with children. Much of the counseling ministry of the church is centered in the needs and burdens of single persons. When a congregation reaches out in love to those who are hurting, the response is often more than anyone can handle.

We at Prince of Peace have a long way to go. We do not respond to human need as quickly as we should, and often people who are hurting get lost in our midst. But we are strongly committed to being a healing community, where both singles and marrieds can find acceptance and growth and love. Through Starting Over Single we hope to welcome in Jesus' name those going through divorce, and to offer strong support. It reflects our understanding of Jesus Christ and the Gospel. We certainly would commend this ministry to singles of your church as well.

CHAPTER ONE

# Divorce

THE NOISE OF THE TELEPHONE shattered the silence of a Sunday afternoon. At the other end of the line a sobbing voice echoed the haunting words, "This is Mary. John has just left us. John has taken all the things he could pile in his car and moved out of the house. He says he is never coming back." What a shock! The pastor was dumbfounded. Their friends were totally surprised. What had seemed to be a happy marriage was now to become another statistic. Two people who had been together for fifteen years were now about to start over single.

The story was so sad and so familiar. Mary talked about what had happened from her own perspective: "John changed. He was not the same person that I married. He was not happy with the friends we had together. He was spending an increasing amount of time with a faster crowd." In fact, he had been doing more drinking both outside and inside the home. Mary had challenged him on his drinking, but John would only become very defensive and upset. When he was drinking, he had become abusive to Mary and the children. The home had become a place of tension and strife.

John seemed to resent his family, according to Mary. It seemed to be an interruption of his real life. His work became the primary focus of his life, and he spent most of his time away from home. He did not want to go to church as often anymore, and he did not seem to care much about communicating with Mary. Just the day before he left, he admitted he was having an affair with a woman from his office.

Mary was shattered by this revelation. She suspected that John was not spending all of his time at work, but she really wanted to trust him. Now all of that trust was gone. She was all torn up inside. She had always believed that a happy marriage could be a reality if both of them worked at it, but now that dream was broken. She didn't know what to do because she had never even considered the possibility that she might be in a situation like this.

John shared a different story. He believed that the marriage was a mistake from the very start, that he and Mary were so completely different. He had become all excited about his career and felt that Mary had little or no interest in what he was doing. She was content to stay home with the children in a world he likened to a "cocoon". "Her whole life became wrapped up in children, curtains and soaps. She hardly even knew that I was around. I wanted to find some excitement, meet some new friends, go to parties, but she never wanted to go with me. So I went alone."

John shared how Mary had become such a negative person. "She was always criticizing me for something. She said I drank too much, I worked too much, I didn't spend enough time with the children, I was not a very good Christian. She kept coming on as this saint who was being forced to live with this terrible sinner.

"So about this time I found there was a woman at work with whom I could communicate, who would really listen to me. We spent many hours just talking. I never dreamed that this would lead to some kind of sexual involvement, but it just seemed to happen. She is also married but is going to move out in a few days. I believe that we are much more suited for each other, and that I will be much happier with her than with Mary."

Many attempts were made to try to convince John that he was making a mistake, that life was not greener on the other side of the fence. There was much discussion about his drinking, but he denied there was any real problem. He blamed Mary for causing him to drink. Many friends of John and Mary tried to convince John to change his mind, but it was to no avail. Meanwhile, Mary quickly decided that life was much more pleasant and peaceful with John gone. She made it clear that since John had walked out, he could just keep right on walking. She didn't even want to see him again.

The next few months were not at all pleasant. Mary had a tremendous anger toward John and especially toward his new woman friend. She wanted to punish both of them in any way that she could. She believed she had "right" on her side, and she was going to receive her pound of flesh. John could not understand her attitude. He wanted bygones to be bygones. He believed that all of the good times that he and Mary had experienced in the past would overshadow these latest events. How mistaken and naive he was!

John had believed that life would not change all that much. He would still drop in very often and mow the lawn, wash the windows, take out the garbage and play with the kids. All that would change would be his address and his sleeping partner. But Mary had radically different ideas. She didn't want him around at all. She didn't want the children seeing their father, especially with the new woman friend present, but the court did not give her this option. It was a period of bitterness, anger, grief, hurt and pain. The court appearances were a living hell. It would take many years to find true healing.

So divorce came into the lives of John and Mary and their children. It had not been planned, was never anticipated, and was not wanted. But one day their marriage became intolerable, and when it fell apart no one was able to put it back together again. Two more people had to start over single.

*Divorce.* How that word drives panic into so many! The very sound of that word gives us an image of a tearing apart, of a ripping sensation. Its spelling appears similar to such words as *divide* or *division*. It also sounds alarmingly like the word *force*, which implies something that is not wanted, that is coerced. We often strive to find another word to describe this phenomenon, one which is less harsh: separated, formerly married, suddenly single.

*Divorce.* It is the end of a dream. Somewhere deep inside of most married persons (and many single persons) is a dream of a family together, of living life happily ever after in love and unity until "death do us part." There is the dream of living for another person, of beautiful love and caring and intimacy. It is a wonderful dream, spoken of in glowing and loving terms at a wedding ceremony by persons who mean it from the very essence of their beings. But now the dream has died, shattered, and has been replaced by a nightmare. Dreams like these never die easily. Nor do marriages.

*Divorce.* The final curtain often falls in a courtroom, but the end happened a long time before. It is legally mandated by some public official, but divorce does not truly take place on a piece of paper. Rather, it happens painfully in the lives and experiences of two persons who are no longer one, who have lost the capacity to be for each other what was promised. A husband and wife often say, "We do not believe in divorce," but whether they believe in it or not, this is what has happened to them. The marriage is over, even if they continue to reside in the same house.

*Divorce.* In the book of Malachi we are told that God hates divorce (Mal. 2:16). There is not a one of us who would disagree. Those who hate it the most are those who have been through it, who know about the pain and sorrow. It is not God's intention that marriages should fail. God intends for all persons to live in harmony and mutual love. Divorce shatters

God's great gift of marriage. It brings tears to the eyes of God when we suffer all of this pain and disharmony. Divorce is tragic. There are no winners in divorce. Everyone loses.

*Divorce.* God is on the side of reconciliation. God does not give up marriages as easily as we do. The Christian community reflects the healing spirit of God by trying to do all that is possible to bring about re-union, recommitment and wholeness in marriage. Very often two persons who have become estranged can find the reconciliation that they seek. We strongly encourage persons contemplating divorce to try everything possible to save their marriages: counseling, therapy, Alcoholics Anonymous, Al-Anon, other classes, whatever it takes. We never want to give up on marriage when there is the slightest breath of life.

*Divorce.* Tragically, however, there are times when nothing is possible anymore except divorce. There is no hope. One or more of the partners has been abused and devastated. The use of chemicals may have become addictive. Abandonment is a reality. A third person has driven a wedge. We continue to believe that with God all things are possible, but these two battered and bruised persons are at the end of the rope. It is over. All we can do is cry. And grieve. And seek to find ways to go on with life, to start over again.

*Divorce.* One purpose of this book is to admit the tragedy of divorce. We understand there is no such thing as pain-less divorce, especially if there has been strong love and commitment. Nor is there any such thing as no-fault divorce. Those who see the brave smiles and confident manner of the divorcing person should be aware that this is just an outward show. Under the mask lies an abundance of sorrow and heartache.

*Divorce.* This book proclaims that divorce is not the end of life. Sometimes it seems that way, but God does not abandon those who hurt. Divorce is not the unforgivable sin. Rather, all of the scriptural evidence shows that God is most truly present for those who are in need. The Gospel of Christ is the good news of forgiveness. The Holy Spirit is going about the work of helping us find new life, of helping us start over again. Divorce is never the final word.

*Divorce.* All are victims. All. Husbands, wives, children, grandparents, brothers and sisters, friends, the church, society as a whole. Victims do not need more abuse. This is a strong statement that needs to be heard by all persons in the church, those who claim to be Christian. The victims of divorce do not need more abuse, especially from people who follow our Lord. Rather, victims of divorce need unconditional love, understanding, care and hope. Jesus described this kind of love in many of his parables and showed it most completely on the cross. Jesus became a victim to give forgiveness and resurrection and new life to all other victims. Divorce is never the final word.

## WHY DO MARRIAGES BREAK DOWN?

Divorce breaks into our world for many reasons. Sometimes it takes place as the inevitable conclusion of a terribly long time of conflict. It is the last nail in the coffin of a dead marriage. Other times it comes as suddenly as a thief in the night. There are as many reasons for divorce as there are marriages. There is really nothing very new in our world in terms of the causes of divorce. Every marriage has circumstances and events within it that create the potential to either build up or tear apart. There is no marriage which could not shatter. What has been given to us for such good can be used instead for such evil.

It might be helpful to look at some of the most common reasons for the breakup of marriages:

1. The abuse of chemicals. A later chapter will be devoted to a more complete discussion of this issue. It is clear to many who are involved in marriage counseling that the abuse of chemicals, particularly alcohol, causes more breakups and problems than any other single reason. It can be the addiction of either the husband or the wife, or both. Or it can be the result

of the addiction of the parent or parents of one of these marriage partners. Chemical abuse in our culture seems at times to be at almost epidemic proportions, and the toll that it is taking on marriages is beyond comprehension.

2. Marriage for the wrong reason. Not all marriages are made in heaven. Some persons should never have married each other. This does not mean that these persons do not believe in marriage or are less than respectable persons. It means they should not have married each other. Some persons marry in order to leave home, to escape from an oppressive living situation, or simply to overcome loneliness. Sometimes a person is looking for a spouse to take care of him or her, to replace the role of the parent. Some marry addictive spouses in order to satisfy some unconscious inner need to nurture or enable.

When persons marry for the wrong reasons, relationships frequently deteriorate rapidly. This often happens to persons who marry between the ages of 18 and 21. There is a vast difference between the maturity of the person who is 18 and the person who is 21. Most marriages that take place between teenagers do not survive these years of growing up. However, there is no age group which is immune to this situation. Many persons marry for the wrong reasons.

3. Changes in people. Men and women marry most often in order that some of their needs might be met. Not all needs can be satisfied within marriage, just some of them, and often most persons are not very aware of what all of these needs might be. Perhaps they feel powerless. For this reason they marry someone who is very strong, so this strength might somehow be transmitted to them. Or they feel the need to be more spiritual, and they turn to a partner who has a strong sense of faith and spirituality. Or they feel the need most of all for someone to understand them and listen to them, so they find someone who has great patience and empathy.

But then their needs change. And quite often the very traits in another person which were so attractive now drive them away. The person they admired for strength is now perceived as coercive. The spouse revered for spiritual commitment, whom they put on a pedestal, is now seen as self-righteous and "holier than thou." The person who was so appealing because of a quiet and serene manner is now upsetting to them as passive and passionless. Human beings are constantly changing. Many times they have changed dramatically and grown apart rather than together. This is especially true when they are unaware of the changes occurring inside of them.

4. Abuse. We are beginning to be sensitive to the widespread tragedy of abuse, especially in the midst of the family. Physical abuse, sexual abuse, and verbal abuse are all too common in marriages and families. Battered women shelters have become commonplace. We need to declare that all abuse is destructive to marriage. It is an effort to destroy, to tear down, to demean. No husband or wife need stay in a marriage where abuse has become a way of life. God did not give us the gift of marriage that we might be destroyed, but rather that we might be given life and love.

5. Growing apart, not together. Every person is either growing, becoming, moving forward, or dying, suffering from apathy, giving up. We do not stay the same. Because of the great range of responses we have toward life, very often marriage partners grow away from each other. In the past it has often been the husband who has been growing, challenged by the job to become more than he is, to expand his horizons. Meanwhile, his wife often has been at home, relating to small children and taking care of the housework. Points of contact have diminished, and both have found the world of the other to be uninteresting and without much meaning.

In more recent times, often the reverse has taken place. Many women are now changing more than men; they are on the cutting edge of growth. Oftentimes growth takes place in the work world or in some kind of educational or volunteer setting. While the wife is greatly expanding her potential and possibilities, the husband often remains static and unchanging. When husband and wife grow together, it can greatly enhance the marriage; when they grow apart, it can be a prelude to divorce.

6. A third person. There is a colorful poster which pictures four large cows in a pasture. Each cow is separated by a barbed wire fence and has very lush and beautiful grass on which to graze, but each cow has her head through the fence into the field of another. There is the temptation today among marriage partners to believe that life might be better somewhere else, with someone else. The grass is greener, the experience more rewarding and exciting with another person. Trade in that worn-out spouse for a new model. There is some mountaintop experience we are missing, and we had better move quickly while we are young enough to do something about it. Often that excitement is found most readily in some forbidden fruit, in that person who looks very good to us outside of marriage. Infidelity does not always lead to divorce, but it surely puts many hurting spouses such as Mary into that kind of a mood.

7. Children. The situation seems a bit ironic that while many children today are being ignored and abandoned by parents, countless others have become the reason and purpose for the marriage. The relationship between husband and wife falls way down on the priority list because most of the energy and time goes into fulfilling the needs or wants of the children. Nothing is too good for our children, no distance too great to drive, no amount of money too exorbitant to spend on them. We want to meet any need or any perceived need. Parents often end up in bondage to their children. They have no life together. They share the same children but very little else.

8. Religion. Above all, our religous beliefs and practices are meant to bring us together, to unify. "There is neither male nor female... you are one in Christ Jesus" (Gal. 3:28). However, more often than we care to admit, faith and spirituality drive us apart rather than together. Our religious journeys are so

different, and we find it hard to relate at this level. One partner may be much more interested in spiritual matters than the other, and this can crate separation. Or there are two religious traditions reflected in a marriage, for example Roman Catholic and Protestant, and at times the problems created seem to be insurmountable. The potential for rift in the area of religion is never very far away.

9. Vocation. Many of us find our sense of self-identity in our work, in the profession we have chosen. In the past this was essentially the domain of the husband but today, with a majority of women working outside the home, it is a reality that confronts both partners. It is very tempting to become almost married to one's work, and this makes it exceedingly difficult for one's partner to share at all in that part of the other's life. Friends at work seem to be competing with the spouse for time and energy and loyalty to the marriage.

Sometimes a marriage cannot stand the strain of a job loss. Also, two-career marriages are under increasing strain because of the demands of the workplace.

10. Lack of communication. This catch-all phrase weaves in and out of all the problems listed above, but it needs specific mention. Too often communication is a victim of our hectic way of life. We only have time to share while on the run. We only talk together in front of the television. We only relate sexually when we are exhausted. We only truly listen when there is a crisis. Communication with one another becomes part of the leftovers, pursued when all of the other more pressing needs are met. Then one day husbands and wives wake up as strangers to each other, ships passing in the night. They have so much in common — a marriage, a place to live, perhaps children, a history — but yet there now seems to be nothing in common. They are very much alone together.

The reasons for divorce are beyond the major thrust of this book, but it may be helpful to consider those listed above. However, what we primarily want to concentrate on in the remainder of these pages is the divorce experience itself: how to understand it, how to see it from a Christian perspective, how to live through it, and how to find resources to start over again. Those who are divorcing have so many questions and sometimes few answers. Now what? Is there life after divorce? Is there any hope for the future? Where is God in my hurt? Why am I so sad? The questions continue to flood their spirits. We now shall turn to some of these questions and seek to find some way of answering them.

CHAPTER TWO

# Divorce is a Death

Divorce Is Like a Death. Something within us has died; something outside of us has gone. The most important relationship we have had as an adult is now over. The dream of our life, the self-portrait we have painted for ourselves, the self-identity we have assumed as married persons — all this has been taken away. Divorce is a death. Many say it is even worse than a death because at this time of death, at this event called divorce, we have not found any acceptable way to grieve.

At the time of an actual physical death of a spouse, the church and society have created a most effective process of response and concern. Family and friends rush to the home which has experienced the death, reaching out to embrace those who are grieving. It is most often a wonderful time of support where people reach out in love to weep with those who weep, who by their very presence give amazing strength and compassion. The pastor often comes to offer spiritual counsel and support, scripture and prayer. Food pours in from all sorts of places, and if there are children who need watching, there are babysitters galore.

## DIVORCE IS A DEATH

If there is a time for visitation at a funeral home, these same people will gather with members of the family, stand by them next to the casket, and bring love and empathy to those in the depths of sorrow. The Christian community then worships together at the funeral, prays with and for the family, and walks with them to the grave.

In the weeks following the funeral, people continue to reach out in many supportive ways: touching, listening, praying, caring. As a church we are fairly effective most of the time in responding to others at the time of an actual physical death. It is one of our most important responsibilities and opportunities to live out the gospel.

Divorce is also a death. But it is abundantly clear that we have not developed any comparable way of grieving. When the separation takes place, when the reality begins to sink in that the marriage is over, there is usually no rush of friends to visit and to mourn. The pastor often does not come. There is even a strong possibility that the pastor is totally unaware of what has taken place. There is nothing even remotely similar to the process of grieving at the time of a death — no visitation, no funeral, no burial. Most often no one is bringing food or offering other kinds of help. As one divorced person commented, "There isn't anyone bringing casseroles to the courthouse." Most often the person going through divorce is completely alone. And when you are alone at a time of the death of a marriage, you are really alone. You know what it means to be abandoned.

Unfortunately, instead of people coming to be with the one who is going through a divorce, the opposite is often true. People back off and stay away from those who have gone through this kind of death. Parents often back off from their children, just when they are needed the most. Neighbors back away from neighbors and good friends withdraw from the situation out of fear of taking sides.

What makes the whole situation still more painful is that

the "corpse" is still walking around, perhaps picking up the children every other week, flooding the other spouse with many painful and searing memories.

Often at a time of the death of a marriage, no one comes. Often when the pain is the greatest, no one is close to share that pain. It is very difficult to experience an actual death of a spouse, but people very seldom do that alone. How different divorce so often is! We need to remember that any death is almost unbearable when we must grieve alone.

Because divorce is a death, the death of a marriage, there are certain things that happen to those who are grieving. Feelings are not the same for everyone. We are still very much individuals, but most of the feelings and experiences listed below happen at some time to those going through divorce. The order may be different and the intensity on a different scale for different people. However, we need to remember that we cannot short-circuit the grieving process. At any time of loss, it is very normal and natural to grieve. The remainder of this chapter will suggest some characteristics that are common to the grief process.

1. Shock. At the time of death or divorce, often we go immediately into shock. This means that we become numb all over; it is almost impossible to feel anything at all. We are so overwhelmed that we cannot comprehend what is happening. We are in a fog. Shock seems to be God's way of protecting us from the full impact of this tragedy. We are disoriented, out of touch with reality, unable to make decisions or take responsibility for much of anything. Shock is a state of disbelief, an inability to accept what has happened to us. We may be as speechless as if we were struck by a thunderbolt.

Shock is sometimes accompanied by a number of physical symptoms. We may have a queasy stomach or feel a sharp pain in our abdomen. We truly hurt inside, and sometimes the pain is almost too much to bear. Our heads may be throbbing or pounding, and we may have a cottony feeling in our mouths.

We may be at a loss concerning our surroundings; we don't know where we are. We have to fight for a sense of equilibrium. We may even lose our appetite. We cannot sleep. How long this time of shock will last varies from person to person, but it usually is present from a few hours to a few days. If shock continues to be with us much longer than that, it is often a sign that we are not moving on as we should, and we should find some kind of professional help.

2. Denial. Shock and denial are very closely related. When the marriage falls apart, when we experience this kind of death, we cannot grasp what has happened. We unrealistically believe that when we wake up the next day, our spouse will be back with us and the nightmare will be over. We live in a world of delusion and make-believe. We may continue to wear our wedding rings, we may sign our Christmas letters and cards with both names, and we may not tell friends and family what has happened. We try desperately to hide this awful reality from others and even from ourselves. We deny the truth.

We may try to live a life of denial by putting on the attitude of unconcern, hoping to convince others that we are very strong and that the divorce has not bothered us all that much. We act like nothing has happened. We want to show others that we have overcome this adversity with just a minimum of pain. As Simon and Garfunkel sing, "We are a rock, an island, and a rock feels no pain." We suggest to others how relieved we are that it is all over. We smother all feelings of loss and pain. This common scenario recalls the words of the poster, "Have you ever told a lie so often that even you begin to believe it?" Denial is living a lie.

3. Emotional overload. Human beings are very resilient. We can handle much of what happens to us. We are very good at coping with what comes our way, but there are times when what comes is just too much. There is a bombardment of our senses that is overwhelming. Our emotions are flooded, similar

to the earth being deluged with many inches of rain in a short period of time. We cannot handle all of the "water," the pain, the hurt. We have the tendency in times like these to hold the feelings inside, to make ourselves sick, to try to tough it out on our own. All sorts of bad things can happen to us when we stuff those feelings deep inside. Ulcers, heart problems, high blood pressure and other physical problems can emerge.

The best way to deal with emotional overload is to get the feelings out: to cry, to beat on a pillow or punching bag, to yell and scream. It is often helpful to talk to someone whom you trust. Emotions need to be released, to be let go. It is okay to feel, to express our feelings, to remember how Jesus wept at his own time of grief. Women are usually much more free to cry, and maybe this is why they live seven or eight years longer than men and are healthier as they become older. Men leran from a very early age that "big boys don't cry." We need to allow ourselves permission to cry. All of us. Chaplain Bill Miller says there exists within us a natural tendency to express feelings. The Creator made us that way. Be natural then; let the emotions flow!

4. Disappointment and failure. Divorce brings to most persons who go through this experience a tremendous feeling of disappointment. They have tried everything in their power to save this marriage but were unable to do so. There is a source of much embarrassment accompanied by a strong sense of personal failure. It is easy to underestimate these feelings of disappointment or deny they exist.

Often the disappointment comes not only from within ourselves but also from those who are close to us. Children, parents, other family members and friends readily communicate to us how disappointed they are in us. "You let us down; how could you do such a thing!" is conveyed in many different ways. We sense that we have brought disgrace, severe disappointment and shame to those around us. This may or may not be true, but the feelings are with us nevertheless. Feeling this way is a natural part of grieving.

    5. Fear. A time of death is a fearful time. What now? What will the future bring? What if I lose control? What if I am unable to handle all of this? There seems to be at the time of divorce the fear among many that they simply will not be able to cope. Perhaps they are crazy, perhaps some kind of mental illness has set in and taken over, maybe there is something seriously wrong with them. Life seems to be so unmanageable. Fits of crying and anger come when they are least expected and when they are least appreciated. Bill Miller calls it "torn and frightened within". This is a normal part of the grieving process. A person going through divorce is not going crazy, is not losing it all, but is just in a temporary and transitional stage.

    6. Anger. It is very hard for us to accept anger in another person. Angry people are frightening. We want to stop others from being so frightening, so we try to convince people to abandon their anger. However, anger is the emotional lifeblood of the grieving person; it can be a definite plus sign on the road to recovery. There is a time to be angry whether the reasons for that anger are clear or not. We can be very angry at the rejection or the perceived rejection that we have experienced. We can be angry about the bad memories that continue to flood our minds and hearts. We can be angry about the sense of abandonment that we feel. All of this even may trigger memories of our childhood, as we remember when we were rejected or abandoned by a boyfriend or girlfriend.

    One of the most difficult things about divorce is that our failure, our pain, has become public knowledge. It is hung out there on the line for all to see. It is bad enough to go through humiliation in private, but to see it has become common knowledge can make us extremely defensive and angry. We have now become a statistic, a fatality, a part of the court record. Our privacy has been violated. We can thus become very angry at our ex-spouse, at ourselves, at a third party, or even at God.

However, it is far better to admit the anger and to express it. We need to get it out, to ventilate the feeling. Feelings of anger are very normal and natural, although there are most definitely appropriate and inappropriate ways of expressing these feelings.

7. Depression. When we turn our anger inward, when we become angry with ourselves, quite often we become depressed. As we have already mentioned, normal anger can be a very healthy emotion. It can foster a release of tension and pain. Depression is usually unhealthy. It has been called the most dangerous dynamic of the grief process. Some depression is normal, but continued depression, a sense of always running uphill and a "what's the use" attitude, can be harmful.

Depression often lowers our resistance to physical illness. It can be an attempt to run away from reality. Sometimes people who are depressed even give up on life or make themselves sick. Depression is like a swimmer in trouble. Struggling is apt to result in drowning, but relaxing and allowing the body to do what is natural will result in automatic surfacing. Self-pity and self-blame at a certain point tear us down. If we continue to be depressed, if we cannot rise up from the depths, then it is most important that we see a competent and compassionate counselor or join a support group where we can gain release and support.

8. Dependency. A person who is in the midst of grief will often want to give someone else power to make decisions for him or her. There is the strong sense that, "This death is just too much for me to bear. I will give another person power to tell me what I should do." At a time of grief, it is easy to become dependent on another. It is so tempting to find an affirmation of our own worth from others. However, when we are dependent, we are easily misled. It is especially important that we do not let this need for dependency push us into some kind of romantic involvement during the grief process. It is most important that we walk through this grief process before

we move on with a new relationship. It is essential that we find a spirit of independence before we find another person with whom we wish to create a new kind of dependency.

9. Sadness. Going through a divorce often brings out in us a surprising sense of sadness. We sometimes are not prepared for this, but one day we discover that we are incredibly sad. There is a profound sense of loss. The marriage may have been destructive for many years, and it is clear that life is better after divorce, but still there is this strong sense of emptiness. This is not unusual, for much has been lost. There is the loss of the life together, the common history, the mutual friends, the many good memories. To grieve is to be aware of this sense of loss and to recognize the sadness that comes. Again, this is normal. Such feelings will come and go through the divorce experience.

In summary, divorce is like a death. Those whose lives have been split apart are grieving persons. We cannot ignore these feelings, we cannot eliminate them, we cannot short-circuit the process. The only way to go through grief is to grieve. God has experienced profound grief and understands fully what we feel. Express the emotions, feel the feelings, and communicate honestly with those who are supportive, but get ready to move beyond the grief process. To start over single always is to grieve first and then move on to the future with hope and expectation.

CHAPTER THREE

# An Understanding of God

$A$ Recent Book Title Asks the question, *Where is God When It Hurts*? We might also ask the related question today, "Where is God in divorce?" Or an even more basic question comes to all of us, whether we are divorced or not, "What is our understanding of God? How do we picture God?"

This may be the most important issue that is dealt with in this book. How we understand God shapes who we are, how we see the world, how we look at ourselves, how we deal with success and failure, and above all, what we see as our purpose here on earth. It is regrettable today that we talk so little about God, and when we do talk about God we neglect to ask the most important question, "What kind of a God do we have?"

Perhaps we should not be so concerned with this question. A recent Gallup poll reported that some 95% of all the adults in the United States believe in God. It could be argued that this is not even an issue. Gallup has proved that we are indeed a nation "under God."

Unfortunately, Gallup neglected to ask the most important and most basic question: In what kind of God do Americans

## AN UNDERSTANDING OF GOD

believe? What is our understanding of God? It does not take too much of a study of history to see how the wrong picture of God has led to all sorts of tragic consequences. A distorted understanding has led to hatred, intolerance, violence and oppression. We may be surprised at this, but if we believe God to be a harsh, oppressive tyrant, it is not much of a step before many followers also will try to be like that image.

As we look at divorce, the perception, the feelings, the image we have of God is much more than academic or theoretical. It can be truly life-giving or life-destroying. If, for instance, we see God to be an angry judge, ready and willing to clobber anyone who falls off the track, then divorce can shake our very foundations. If we see God as an absentee landlord, off doing other things, unconcerned about the mundane details of our life, then we may be in a period of aloneness which is terrifying.

But if God is seen primarily as love, as forgiveness, as hope, this can paint a picture of beauty centered in hope. If we can see within the heart of God that there is a cross, then our perspective has been radically changed. If we can look very closely at Jesus' life and teachings, death and resurrection, then we can find for ourselves that nothing can take us away from the love of God. If we find in God the one who cares deeply about those who hurt, we can discover the resources to begin all over again.

What is our picture of God, our basic understanding? The Sunday School teacher noticed a little girl in her class drawing a picture. "What are you drawing?" the teacher asked. "Oh," said the little girl, "I am drawing a picture of God." "A picture of God," exclaimed the teacher, "but no one knows what God looks like." "Well," said the little girl, "they will as soon as I finish my picture."

The Bible is full of word pictures, and many of these pictures are specifically of God. There are far too many of these verbal snapshots to feature in a book, but there are several that might be especially helpful to those who are confronting the reality of divorce. These images and descriptions of God touch the lives of everyone in our world but seem to be highly relevant to those who are suddenly single. They give a very definitive "yes" to all who wonder if there is any life after divorce.

We will examine four pictures of God in this chapter.

## GOD IS LIKE A PARENT

This is one of the favorite themes in the Bible because it is so understandable. God is like a parent. This should not be at all surprising, for it certainly seems logical that we should take the closest relationship we can have here on this earth and use this human language to describe our closeness with our Creator.

From the first breath we take, we have a closeness and unity with those who gave us birth. Not only are we given the gift of life and the nurture that is needed, but also we are given the beautiful gifts of unconditional love and acceptance by our parent or parents. Most often there is a sense of compassion and closeness that cannot be overestimated. The image of God as a parent gives us an excellent picture of God.

Martin Luther, in his explanation to the First Article of the Creed in the Small Catechism, uses many parenting words to describe God. Luther is trying to paint word pictures. God has "given to me and still preserves my body and soul with all their powers. He provides me with food and clothing, home and family, daily work, and all that I need from day to day. God also protects me in time of danger and guards me from every evil." All of this portrays for us the picture of a parent and children.

The most common picture of God in terms of a parent is that of a father. This has been a strongly influential picture for many of us, and we demonstrate this most often when we pray, "Our Father, who art in heaven." Jesus very often calls upon God as his father. For the most part, this image of God as father has been very helpful. However, where persons have

## AN UNDERSTANDING OF GOD

suffered in family situations from an abusive or an absent father, this image sometimes has not been very constructive.

Perhaps the most moving look at God as a father is found in Jesus' parable of the prodigal son, Luke 15:11-32. The younger son asked one day for his inheritance, and upon receiving this substantial gift he went a long distance away. In his new place of residence life quickly deteriorated. It is entirely possible that he was married and divorced, and it is also very likely that he was an alcoholic. Hitting bottom as he did in a pigpen sounds very familiar to many alcoholics.

One day the son woke up with nothing, no person close to him, no self respect, nothing. He was devastated and wanted more than anything else to go home again. He returned, not knowing if his father would even want to see him. He came prepared to repent and to become a servant. When he was still a distance away, his father saw him and ran out to meet him. The father embraced his son, kissed him, put a ring on his finger and a robe on his back. A wonderful celebration took place.

Jesus makes it abundantly clear that God is like this father. No person can go too far away, or live so badly, or reject the father so completely that he or she cannot be welcomed back again. God is like a father who sees his child in deep pain and heartache, whose love is unconditional and eternal. God is like a father who will never stop loving, never stop forgiving, never stop waiting for his child to come home again.

There are also many instances in the Bible where God is pictured as being like a mother. This may surprise us, for such emphasis has not received very much attention, but when we give this some thought, it should make good sense to us. If God is like a parent, then that picture should very naturally include both father and mother. Parenting is very clearly the gift given to both male and female, and it is a theme that is picked up by many biblical writers. When we see God as like both a father and a mother, it widens and broadens our understanding of God and enhances our total picture.

Perhaps the most illustrative material of God as a mother is found in Hosea 11:3-4: "Yet I was the one who taught Israel to walk. I took my people up in my arms, but they did not acknowledge that I took care of them. I drew them to me with affection and love. I picked them up and held them to my cheek; I bent down to them and fed them." (GNB)

Here we have a beautiful picture of a mother, a loving parent who is nurturing, feeding, holding her child close. It is clear in the biblical picture that there is a relationship between a mother and a child that a father will never completely experience. In carrying the child inside of her, in giving birth, in giving primary nurture, there is a closeness and unity that is unparalleled. The experience of a mother is unique, and yet this is the kind of relationship between a parent and child that is descriptive of God. God is like a mother.

This is why in Deuteronomy 32:18 God says to the people of Israel, "You were unmindful of the Rock that begot you, and you forgot the God who gave you birth." God is the one who gives birth to people like us. This describes a mother.

The words of Isaiah 49:14-15 say, "But Zion said, 'The Lord has forsaken me, my Lord has forgotten me.' Can a woman forget her suckling child, that she should have no compassion on the son of her womb?" In other words, how can God, who is like a mother, ever forget her child no matter how far that child has strayed? How can God, who is like a mother, ever forget, ever lose compassion for her child?

To summarize, God is pictured in very emphatic terms as being like a parent. We must always be aware that our human language can never create a complete description of God. God is far beyond any human understanding, yet the picture of the parent is a very helpful one.

As a parent, God loves, gives birth, nurtures, sustains, protects, disciplines, forgives, provides and heals. For those

## AN UNDERSTANDING OF GOD

who have been divorced, who are suffering any kind of pain, God is like a parent. For all those who hurt, God is waiting with outstretched arms, with a heart full of compassion and a spirit of unconditional acceptance and love.

### GOD IS AFFECTED BY WHAT HAPPENS TO US

Sometimes it is very tempting to believe that God is not personally involved with us. Sometimes we tend to picture God as being remote, out there, one who has created this world and then moved on to other galaxies and planets. But the biblical word about God is that God is as close to us as our very breath, that God never takes a vacation, never leaves us alone, never is removed from our pain and joy.

God is not only very close to us but also deeply affected by what happens to us. The impact of this declaration is hard even to comprehend, but this is what the biblical authors assert again and again. Exodus 2:23-25 is a good example of this truth: "The people of Israel groaned under their bondage, and cried out for help... and God saw the people of Israel, and knew their condition." The word "knew" in the Bible is a very intimate word. God "knew" the sufferings of the people, which means that he entered into that suffering in a most intimate way.

In Isaiah 16:9 we see the very graphic picture of God with tears, anguishing over the world and the suffering of the people. It would not be very difficult today to make a case for this being a most appropriate picture for this period of history, a God with tears. With so much pain around us and in us, with the explosive rise in divorce, God must be filled with tears. What happens to us deeply impacts God.

Prayer gives us some insight into this understanding of God. Time and again in the Bible the prayers of the people impact God; God is moved and affected by the prayers. In fact, there are numerous instances where God's mind is even changed by prayer. God is not the unmoved mover. We cannot accept the words of the Protestant reformer, John Calvin, who stated, "Nothing sad or sorrowful can happen to God, who remains untouched."

God is affected by what happens to the world and to us. Prayer makes a difference to God and also to us. God weeps with those who weep and rejoices with those who rejoice.

## God's Power Is a Self-giving, Suffering Power

It is sometimes easy to think of God only as power. God is almighty, all powerful, as mighty as anything in the whole world, only more so. God is in control of everything and can do anything. So when a marriage falls apart and God doesn't save it, or when a child is hit by a car and God doesn't prevent it, we don't know what in the world to say. If God has all this power, why doesn't God step in?

The message of the Scriptures, and one which is in some sense impossible for us to truly comprehend, is that God has chosen to limit this great power. Somehow, from the very beginning there was in the heart of God a cross. God could have addressed the world with absolute power, "You do as I say or else." Some followers even today attempt to picture God in these terms.

However, it is clear especially in the life of Jesus Christ that God has chosen to use this awesome power in terms of suffering. In many instances, Jesus was exhorted to bring down the power of God upon the world, to "zap" someone who was being an obstacle in the way of the kingdom. But Jesus understood this power in a radically different way; he saw it primarily in terms of suffering. This is why Paul wrote these words, "Jesus emptied himself, taking the form of a servant." Instead of riding the white horse of earthly power on Palm Sunday, Jesus rode on a donkey, the symbol of emptiness and humility.

The message is that God has chosen to suffer for and suffer with those who are experiencing pain. In every way God has been tempted and battered as we have been. We sometimes would like to call upon some kind of absolute power to come

## AN UNDERSTANDING OF GOD

in and supernaturally change the situation or kick out those who make our life miserable. God's power is most evident in weakness and in suffering. This means that our Lord stands in solidarity with those who suffer and feels what we feel. Jesus' life and death are a beautiful picture of a God who cares deeply for the hurting in our midst. We also are called to give up any kind of desire for absolute power, to respond in self-giving love and in servanthood. For those who have been divorced, God knows the pain that is present, the suffering, and God enters into that pain to help bring about a resurrection, a starting over.

### GOD IS WORKING TO LIBERATE THE OPPRESSED

Throughout the Scriptures there is a basic theme at work. God wants to set free all who are in bondage, those persons who are oppressed in any way. Sometimes the religious community has been more on the side of the oppressors, but the God of the Bible always is working for liberation. Persons who are experiencing divorce often know a great deal about oppression and bondage and so need to hear about the God who sets us free.

In the Old Testament is a profound story of the surprising liberation of a very poor and oppressed people. God set his people free. When in later periods of history the people of Israel became oppressors rather than the oppressed, God anguished beyond words. How could anyone who had felt the lash of oppression turn around and become abusers of others? Whenever the people are suffering, whenever they are groaning in pain, then God is close at hand bringing liberation and love and freedom.

Jesus' life and ministry again are instructive. He spent much of his time with the oppressed, the poor, the subordinate in society. He is constantly telling those who think they are nobody that they are somebody. He even takes to himself the words from Isaiah 61 to paint the clearest picture of his ministry:

"The Spirit of the Lord God is upon me, because the Lord has anointed me to bring good news to the afflicted; he has sent me to bind up the brokenhearted, to proclaim liberty to the captives, and the opening of the prison to those who are bound." Jesus then declared, "Today this is fulfilled."

In summary, God is on the side of liberation, of freedom, of mutual respect for one another. God is opposed to all kinds of oppression and bondage and stands with those who have been battered in our world. He reserves the harshest words for the rich and the powerful who are enslaving others and shows the most compassion for those who have been oppressed. God stands with all who are enslaved.

There are many more pictures of God in the Bible, but those discussed in this chapter are among the most significant. It is crucial as each of us struggles with our understanding of God, that we be open to new insights and discoveries. For it is our image of God that will determine and shape many of our attitudes toward life, toward others, and toward ourselves.

Our understanding of God will also impact our response to divorce. A healthy biblical view of God will give us much support and encouragement; the wrong view can tear us apart. We always need to remember that the God of the Bible is primarily a God of good news, compassion, love, forgiveness, liberation. God gives us the resources to start over again, no matter what has happened to us.

CHAPTER FOUR

# The Old Testament and Divorce

WHAT DOES THE BIBLE SAY? This question is of prime concern to most of us. Whenever people gather to discuss the issues of marriage, divorce and remarriage, this question always seems to be at the top of the list. Rightfully so. This is certainly a theological issue. It most assuredly has many serious implications concerning God's intention for us and for the world. To try to deal with divorce without carefully looking at the biblical material would be a very limited approach. Thus, we will attempt to ask the question, "What does the Bible say?"

Right away we have a fundamental problem. The Bible says many things. It did not drop out of heaven one day with one clear answer for every question that would arise. For some questions there seem to be no clear answers, and for other issues that challenge us there seem to be a multitude of answers. There are, of course, many authors who have written in the Bible, and they have come from many different periods in history, perspectives, locations and understandings. Sometimes what is written seems to our finite minds to be rather confusing and unclear, at times even contradictory.

Many very sincere Christian people interpret the same Bible quite differently. This is why we have close to 300 different denominations in the United States, most of which claim to follow the Bible. We do not have to look very far to discover that there is a biblical word to support just about anything we want. If we want a biblical word to support polygamy, look at Abraham, David and Solomon. Wives were as plentiful as the stars in the sky. If we want a biblical mandate for capital punishment, look at the laws of Moses. If we want to find a word to defend the oppression of women or the legalization of slavery, there are numerous verses that can be chosen.

On the other hand, there is also the opposite word to be found in the Bible. There are some very strong words about fidelity in marriage, about faithfulness to one other person. This comes as early as the first chapter of Genesis. There is ample evidence in the Bible to support pacifism as opposed to the death penalty — turn the other cheek, love your enemy, and so on. There are many statements of Jesus and others which give very strong affirmation concerning the dignity and worth and status of women in contrast to the degrading pictures. There are strong words against the oppression of others such as is found in the institution of slavery. So, in essence, we find in the Bible some mixed voices. It is not always clear what the final word of the Bible should be.

Thus, it is important that we approach the Scripture with a very clear understanding of interpretation. What is the essence of the message? If there are different ideas expressed, where do we give the most emphasis? This book will answer those questions with the person of Jesus Christ. In order to understand the Bible, in order to find the authoritative word of God, we will look at the life and teaching and death of Jesus as our authority. In order to most fully understand the ethical and moral issues of that day and our day, it is best that we begin and end with Jesus.

## THE OLD TESTAMENT AND DIVORCE

Jesus is the ultimate picture we have of God. No one has ever taken a camera and snapped a picture of God, but in Jesus Christ we have an earthly, physical, human picture of God. If there are places in the Scripture which seem to be confusing, we must try to interpret these through the message and the example of Jesus. Even in parts of the Bible where Jesus is nowhere to be found physically, we still see his presence and spirit at the center of that teaching. If we ignore that presence, we can come up with a wide variety of teachings and understandings, some of them completely at odds with each other.

For example, if Moses writes that a woman who is caught in adultery should be stoned, but Jesus writes in the sand, "Let the person who is without sin cast the first stone," then it is the conviction of this book that we should follow Jesus and not Moses. If the Old Testament king goes out and kills women and children, but Jesus says we are to turn the other cheek, then the latter is our primary word. If the Apostle Paul writes some words that cause us concern in terms of the status of women, divorce, Holy Communion, or speaking in tongues, or whatever it might be, we need always to see this through the eyes of Jesus. If we understand fully the word of Paul and the message of Jesus there may not be contradictions, but if some of these issues trouble us, then we must begin and end with Jesus.

As we begin with the Old Testament, we discover quickly that there is not much written about divorce in these 39 books. In fact, there are only two major passages which direct themselves toward the response of the Old Testament community to divorce. It is certainly puzzling why there is not more written. After all, there are chapters upon chapters describing how to build a tabernacle but just a few isolated verses about this terribly wrenching social problem in the community. We might wish desperately that more had been written, but we can only discuss what we have been given.

We start at the beginning. It is highly important and

fascinating that when Jesus was asked the crucial question in the book of Mark about divorce, Mark 10:2-12, he went back immediately to the words from Genesis 1 and 2. He could have quoted from Deuteronomy, which we will discuss shortly, or chosen from other frames of reference, but he went right back to the beginning. If we look closely at the biblical accounts of creation, we will discover why he did this. In Genesis 1 and 2 we have the most beautiful, the most profound, the most important words about God's intention for marriage. And we cannot truly talk about divorce until first we have understood the theology of marriage.

In Genesis 1 and 2 it is essential first of all that we see two different accounts of creation. That may be a surprise to many readers because we have for the most part only heard about one. But there are two creation stories. The reason there are two is a subject in itself, and we will not take the time in this book to deal with that. It is enough that we see these two accounts and find how different they are. They are not necessarily in contradiction, but they are very different.

The first account of creation is found in Genesis 1 with the most significant verses being 26 and 27: "Then God said, 'Let us make man in our image, after our likeness; and let them have dominion over the fish of the sea, and over the birds of the air, and over the cattle, and over the earth, and over every creeping thing that creeps upon the earth.' So God created man in his own image, in the image of God he created them; male and female he created them."

We discover that in the beginning God created Adam. In the Hebrew Adam does not mean just one man but humanity, both male and female. God created male and female in Genesis 1. There is no implication that the man was created first. Rather, it implies that man and woman were created at the same time. The word "Adam" really means "earth creature," the "stuff of the earth." Human beings are created to be the crown of God's creation. God saves the best for last and creates male and female

# THE OLD TESTAMENT AND DIVORCE

in his image. Image means likeness. Male and female are created to be like God. This is not completely spelled out, but it is clear that male and female are to be God's sevants, God's children, his reflection in the world.

There is no differentiation in Genesis 1 between male and female, no indication that the male is superior to the female, or that the male comes first. There is no evidence whatsoever that the male is in the image of God and the female is in the image of man, which seems to be so prevalent in later Old Testament teaching. Genesis 1 does not present any kind of emphasis. Genesis 5:1-2 reinforces this interpretation of Genesis 1: "When God created man (Adam), he made him in the likeness of God. Male and female he created them and he blessed them and named them Man (Adam) when they were created."

So the picture of Genesis 1 is that man and woman were created at the very same time, equal partners, both created in the image of God. Male and female are the crown of creation. There is no picture of dominant and subordinate. It is a beautiful picture of partnership, equality, and oneness. It is certainly clear why Jesus returned to these words for a clear understanding of marriage and divorce.

The second account of creation is found in Genesis 2. As mentioned earlier, it is a very different picture. Here the creation of the world takes place in a different order. The heavens and the earth are created first, then the human beings, and then the plants and the animals. Why two creation stories? Once again we are reminded that the Bible was written by many different authors inspired by the Holy Spirit. These authors came out of vastly different traditions, histories and circumstances. Even today we have many different ways of interpreting the same event. I suppose it is not all that surprising to find this in the Bible.

The creation story in Genesis 2 has a major difference. It talks about the male being created first. The man is created first, and then a helper is made for him. We must make sure, however, that we rely on the biblical understanding of the word "helper" rather than Webster's definition. Webster says that the word "helper" implies something close to menial labor, one who is unquestionably subordinate. But the Hebrew word for "helper" means more like "partner". In fact, it is a word that is usually reserved in the Old Testament for God. God is our helper, our partner. With this in mind it is clear that no second class citizenship is implied, for God's relationship to us is hardly subordinate.

After the male is created in Genesis 2, the female is created. Again in this chapter there is no hint of male superiority or female inferiority, no designation of one being more powerful and the other less powerful. There is nothing here about different vocational tasks. Neither of the accounts suggests this. In both Genesis 1 and 2 there is the picture of the male and female in the image of God, together having dominion, stewards of the world. There is the picture of mutuality, of oneness, of complementing each other.

We simply cannot overestimate the problems that have arisen from a mistaken interpretation of Genesis 2. Sometimes theologians (usually male, of course) have suggested that Genesis 2 proves that women are somehow inferior to men because the man was created first. That is hardly what was meant. Once again we are reminded of how easy it is to take almost any verse or text and prove what we want to prove. It is essential here to make sure we look very closely at Jesus Christ, at his life and teaching. It is clear that his understanding of the dignity and worth of women was far different from that of the Old Testament community.

Let's look at an illustration of how we can so easily interpret a passage or chapter to prove a point of view. It is not difficult to see how Genesis 2 could be used to defend male superiority. After all, the man was created first and the woman from his rib. However, it also could be seen in the opposite light. Basically, creation takes place from the lowest form to

## THE OLD TESTAMENT AND DIVORCE

the highest. Thus, if the woman is created last, she would be the crown of creation. As one theologian says with tongue in cheek, "Maybe the man was just a rough draft." Both of these arguments are distortions. Genesis 1 and 2 do not build a case for dominance or subordination of either male or female.

The biblical picture is one of being equal partners, having dominion, taking care of God's world. Men and women are created in the image of God and are created good. They have been created to be in union with each other, one flesh, one spirit. There is to be a sense of wholeness, completeness. It is an expression of complete faithfulness to each other, a picture of shameless, beautiful mystery of God.

There is no thought in Genesis 1 and 2 of this union being broken. This is the ideal, paradise, God's ultimate intention for his people. Any breaking of this bonding, this partnership, is a violation of the sacred purpose of God. God's intention is that male and female should be together until death parts them. There is no room here for anything but total harmony and joy and love.

But the whole thing breaks apart in Genesis 3. Here begin the distortions that have marked the relationships between men and women. It does not come from Genesis 1 and 2 but from Genesis 3. Here is found the picture of the male over the female, husband dominant over the wife. It springs out of the sin and brokenness and disharmony of Genesis 3. Here we find the words about the pain of childbirth and the husband ruling over the wife.

But this is not the ideal, not the intention of God as found in Genesis 1 and 2. This is now a part of the fallen world. We must wonder why we have tended to take so many of our moral attitudes and norms from the sinful condition in Genesis 3, rather than from God's ideal purpose in Genesis 1 and 2. We must wonder why so much of Old Testament life, with its male dominated society, only went back to Genesis 3. We must wonder why today we still end in much the same place. Probably 90% of the books in our Christian bookstores today still talk about domination and subordination, submission and the chain of command. They only go back to Genesis 3. Genesis 1 and 2 knew nothing about these ideas; rather, here is the picture of man and woman together in covenant, equal partners.

Jesus goes directly back to Genesis 1 and 2. He jumps right over Genesis 3, for he wanted to picture again the harmony, the sacred unity that is to be found in marriage. By pointing to this ideal, this beautiful picture of God's intentions, Jesus is painting a picture of what marriage is meant to be. Divorce was never meant to happen. Marriage was meant to be forever. We should never lose sight of this ideal. Even in the midst of much divorce in our world, we still need to be reminded constantly of God's beautiful intention for us, for men and women, for marriage.

The Old Testament is a strong witness to how quickly things went astray. Divorce soon became rampant in Jewish society. One of the major problems was that men had all the power, and women were treated as property. This hardly lent itself to the understanding of unity from Genesis 1 and 2. Without this mutual love and respect, without this sense of partnership, marriage soon became a distortion, an institution which formalized the domination of men and the subordination and even victimization of women. When marriage became so unfair, divorce was inevitable.

Moses must have been confronted with divorce almost as soon as he was given leadership. Again, it is surprising that there is not a good deal more written about divorce. Moses must have spent an inordinate amount of time trying to bring about some semblance of order and ethics in the midst of chaos. Myrna and Robert Kysar, in their excellent book, *The Assundered: Biblical Teachings of Marriage, Divorce and Remarriage*, give the most comprehensive treatment of this biblical material that I have found, and I would strongly recommend this book.

## THE OLD TESTAMENT AND DIVORCE

The primary passage in the Old Testament on divorce is found in Deuteronomy 24:1-4. There are several other references to divorce in the Old Testament, but none of them deal with the basic theme of this book, and so we will not refer to them in this discussion. Let's look at these words from Deuteronomy 24: "When a man takes a wife and marries her, if then she finds no favor in his eyes because he has found some indecency in her, and he writes her a bill of divorce and puts it in her hand and sends her out of his house, and she departs out of his house, and if she goes and becomes another man's wife, and the latter husband dislikes her and writes her a bill of divorce and puts it in her hand and sends her out of his house, or if the latter husband dies, who took her to be his wife, then her former husband who sent her away, may not take her again to be his wife, after she has been defiled; for that is an abomination before the Lord, and you shall not bring guilt upon the land which the Lord your God gives you for an inheritance."

By way of explanation, it is helpful to know that in the Old Testament there are basically two kinds of laws. One is the absolute law, the one which is for everyone, which cannot be broken no matter what. It usually begins with the words, "You shall not," such as we find in the Ten Commandments. Even in these absolute laws, however, there is a strong sense of forgiveness that is promised, and especially as we look at the person of Jesus Christ. No matter how much we break the law, we are never prevented from returning to the love and forgiveness of God. The parable of the prodigal son is a case in point.

But there is another kind of law which we call conditional law. This is a rule or commandment to be applied to a very specific situation. There are many of these laws in the Old Testament. The biblical authors attempted to interpret the absolute laws in terms of very concrete circumstances, as we continue to try to do. Obviously, there are so many millions of variations that can take place that only a relative handful find their way into the Scriptures. It appears that the first four verses of Deuteronomy 24 are such a conditional statement.

We find the conditional statement in the first three verses. If the following events happen — if the man finds indecency in his wife, and if he divorces her, and if she marries another, and if the new husband divorces her or he dies — if all this happens, then the first husband cannot marry her again. There are obviously many other conditions that could have been mentioned and many other statements made, but for some reason this is the only one like it in the Old Testament.

This condition seems more than a little strange to us. It somehow creates the impression that it is much ado about nothing. If a man divorces his wife and then she is remarried and this man either divorces her or dies, then why should the first husband not be able to remarry her? Wouldn't that be better, for instance, than a third husband coming into the picture? It was just not an option in those days for a divorced woman to be self-supporting, so if a woman was divorced by her second husband, would it not be better for her to remarry the first one than to be destitute and vulnerable to whatever came along?

We are not really sure why this law was mentioned. It may have been to discourage a hasty divorce in the first marriage. In other words, what Moses wanted to say to the men of his day was this, "When you are divorced, you had better make sure this is what you want, because you are forbidden to remarry that same woman." It might have been a warning to those who were married to stay that way.

It could have been a way of protecting the second marriage. The first husband might have had second thoughts about this divorce after the fact and might have wanted to bring back his former wife, but this conditional law told him to forget it. It's all over once you have written that divorce decree. You have made your bed. Now you must sleep in it.

It also might have been a law that was to keep the wife in the second marriage from threatening to leave this new husband and run back to the first one. She might have come to the conclusion that the second marriage was not as exciting as the first and wanted to return. This law may have been to keep her from such thoughts. We are not really sure why this conditional law is mentioned.

Another puzzling factor is that this law does not seem to be taken with much seriousness in the Old Testament community. It is clear it does not have anything like the status of the absolute laws. Look, for instance, at II Samuel 3:14-16. King David asks in these verses that his former wife be restored to him. Her husband is dead, but there is no mention here that this might be improper. We can assume that King David and his advisors knew this conditional law from Deuteronomy, and yet it is ignored. A similar situation also takes place in the book of Hosea.

If these words in Deuteronomy 24 had been an absolute law, we could very clearly argue that divorce is mandatory when the conditions described here are present. Let's spell that out again. If the husband finds his wife to be indecent, he is obligated to divorce her. It is most important that we see this as a conditional law, directed at very specific situations. It does not say that divorce is mandatory, or even that it is permissible, but only that it is present and real in the Jewish community. It does suggest that divorced men and women were free to remarry.

There is one part of these verses in Deuteronomy that has created all sorts of problems in later interpretation. It has to do with the use of the word "indecent" or "shameful". "If she finds no favor in his eyes because he has found some 'indecency' in her." What is meant by this? Many have interpreted this to mean adultery. In other words, if a woman commits adultery, then she can be sent out of the home and divorce is legitimate. Unfortunately, it began that process of trying to decide when divorce is biblically all right and when it is not. Here it revolves around the area of indecency.

The Kysars, among others, contend that to equate indecency with adultery is probably a mistake. There were already some very clear laws about adultery, and the penalty for this sin was death. These laws were more absolute than conditional. It is not likely that a man would have divorced his wife if he had discovered she was adulterous. Death would have been a more likely alternative.

Indecency most likely referred to something else, although we are not sure what this was. Perhaps the public behavior of the wife created embarrassment for the husband. Maybe there was some kind of addiction problem here. Maybe it even referred to childlessness, which was a very serious matter in the Old Testament community. It is not at all unreasonable to expect that a husband might divorce his wife if she did not have any children. Perhaps this was the meaning of indecency.

What is clear in Deuteronomy is that divorce is not just the whim of the husband. He cannot put his wife out of the home for no reason, but there must be some kind of indecent behavior on the part of the wife. With this bill of divorce the woman now has a written document proving she has been divorced and has the right to remarry without being charged with adultery. It gives women very minimal rights.

But at the same time it is clear that divorce in the Old Testament is strictly a male privilege. The husband alone could initiate such action. He needed some grounds, although indecency covered such a wide territory, it was almost blanket permission. The divorced woman was then dismissed or sent away, which is the meaning of divorce in that setting.

Let us summarize the writings on divorce in the Old Testament, especially as found in these verses in Deuteronomy. Divorce was clearly allowed and practiced, as well as remarriage. There is no general legislation in the Old Testament regarding either divorce or remarriage. The right to divorce or

## THE OLD TESTAMENT AND DIVORCE

the right to remarry are nowhere officially instituted, nor are they officially forbidden. It is apparent that divorce was widespread in the Old Testament community, but it is also apparent that divorce did not lie easily on the nation's conscience.

Today we as the Christian community must ask the question, "Are the divorce and remarriage customs of the Old Testament Jewish community consistent with God's revelation in Jesus Christ?" We must go back to our interpretive principle. As we look at divorce through the person and teaching of Christ, can we be comfortable with the Old Testament attitude? Was it wrong to allow divorce and remarriage? Is this part of the stuff of the Old Testament, like animal sacrifice and polygamy that we should just discard?

I believe that we should indeed take seriously the teaching of the Old Testament. The Hebrews were very close to the revelation of God. It is instructive for us to find that they believed divorce and remarriage were logical necessities in the kind of world in which they lived. They were well aware that divorce was against the ideal. It was not God's intention. However, they also realized that at times broken and fragile persons had no choice. They knew that marriage sometimes becomes unbearable and is destructive of human dignity. They understood that not every marriage is able to progress toward the beauty and wonder that is described in Genesis 1 and 2.

What does the Bible say about divorce? In the Old Testament not very much is said, at least not enough for us to formulate a complete picture of theological understanding. Now we will turn quickly to the New Testament.

CHAPTER FIVE

# The New Testament and Divorce

The New Testament Does Not Spend much time dealing with divorce. This does not necessarily mean that the issue was unimportant to the Biblical writers but that there are just a few verses that even bring it up. There is ample material about the use of money, or about concern for the poor, or about witnessing for Christ, but there is very little about divorce.

Thus, as we attempt to interpret the teaching of the New Testament, it is important to keep in mind the whole of the Biblical message, not just these few passages. We need to reflect often on our understanding of God, especially as we see it reflected in the life and death and resurrection of Jesus. We are most able to discern the biblical view of divorce by being open to the complete picture of God.

At the time that Jesus began his ministry, divorce was one of those pressing issues that was under some debate. The Pharisees, who were trying to bring the Old Testament law of

## THE NEW TESTAMENT AND DIVORCE

Moses into clearer focus, believed that every man had the right to divorce his wife. They also believed that a woman did not have the same right; in fact, women did not have many rights at all.

The real issue being debated at the time of Jesus is not whether divorce is legal or consistent with the law of God, but under what circumstances divorce can take place. As was mentioned in the discussion of the Old Testament view, divorce was probably very common and accepted at this time, but there was much difference of opinion as to what causes were justified.

The Kysars, in their book, *The Assundered: Biblical Teachings of Marriage, Divorce and Remarriage*, have an excellent discussion of this issue, and I will reflect some of their conclusions in this chapter.

There were two basic positions on divorce that were prominent as Jesus began his ministry. The first was the more liberal approach, led by a Rabbi Hilel. He declared that the Old Testament law on divorce meant that a husband could divorce his wife if she displeased him for any reason. There must be a reason, but this was only playing word games, for the reason could be anything from burning the toast to childlessness.

The other influential school of thought was led by a Rabbi Shammai. His point of view was that in order for divorce to be sanctioned, the woman must be guilty of the indecency we read about in the book of Deuteronomy. Again, this refers only to the wife, not the husband. To this rabbi indecency meant adultery. We mentioned earlier how unlikely this interpretation would have sanctioned the penalty of death for any adulterous behavior, but this was a strong view as Jesus' ministry began.

The problem inherent in this debate was not hard to see. Instead of dwelling on the pain and suffering of those persons whose marriages were in trouble, the emphasis centered on which causes were legitimate. Some were all right and some were not. In other words, some divorces were justified and some were not. This opened a whole arena of mental gymnastics as people tried to make sure that their divorce was justified in the eyes of that society. It is this kind of thinking that later led to the "exemption clauses" we find in both Matthew and the writings of Paul, which were meant to give people a way out. We will look at these more closely later on.

To introduce the words on divorce, it is perhaps helpful to understand the order in which the Gospels were writen. It is believed by most biblical scholars that the Gospel of Mark was written first, that it is oldest among the Gospels. It is believed that both Matthew and Luke depended rather extensively on the book of Mark as they wrote their books. If we would study these three books closely, we would discover that many verses in Matthew and Luke are word for word from the Gospel of Mark. What keeps interpreters very busy is trying to discover what caused Matthew and Luke to change some of that which was written by Mark. We will see this in terms of divorce.

Most scholars believe that Matthew and Luke were writing to quite different audiences. Matthew was writing to a Jewish community and Luke to a gentile population. In targeting their letters for these different groups, they highlight different words and actions of Jesus which might have the most impact on their readers. They were much like preachers today, who select certain passages, certain nuances which can speak most forcefully to the audience. They tell the same story in different ways, seeing quite varied and even contradictory aspects in the same event.

The Gospel of Mark was probably written around 70 A.D. with Luke and Matthew written some years later. Because Mark is our primary source, we will begin here with the discussion of divorce. The basic verses that speak to this issue are found in Mark 10:2-12: "And Pharisees came up and in order to test him asked, 'Is it lawful for a man to divorce his wife?' He answered them, 'What did Moses command you?' They said,

## THE NEW TESTAMENT AND DIVORCE

'Moses allowed a man to write a certificate of divorce, and to put her away.' But Jesus said, 'For your hardness of heart he wrote you this commandment. But from the beginning of creation, God made them male and female. For this reason a man shall leave his father and mother and be joined to his wife, and the two shall become one. So they are no longer two but one. What therefore God has joined together, let not man put asunder.' And in the house the disciples asked him again about this matter. And he said to them, 'Whoever divorces his wife and marries another, commits adultery against her, and if she divorces her husband and marries another, she commits adultery.'"

It is very clear in this passage that Jesus is declaring that there are no exemptions for divorce. Genesis 1 and 2 set up the ideal for marriage, and this is what God has intended for each of us who is married. Divorce is a breaking of the covenant. Moses had compromised and had made exceptions, as in the case of indecency. But as we see in the book of Mark, Jesus declares divorce to be against the will of God for anyone. It is a tragic interruption of what God has joined together.

It does not take long for the exemptions to begin. Jesus' words in Mark allow for no exemptions, but other authors quickly change all that. This is understandable because these authors found in their new churches many people who were wrestling with this issue, and they wanted to provide a way out of a destructive marriage. So Matthew adds the clause of exemption, "There is no place for divorce, except for unchastity." This changes everything. In Mark there is no just cause for divorce, but in Matthew there is an out. Now the struggle begins to define the word "unchastity".

Later on the Apostle Paul will also add an exemption clause. Paul declares that divorce is against the will of God except when one of the partners is an unbeliever. Again, this is not what Mark quotes Jesus as saying, and it is quite different from Matthew. It is really the third exemption that we find:

first, indecency as mentioned by Moses, then Matthew's words on unchastity, and now the admonition about unbelievers.

These exemptions seem to give us too many loopholes. Also, they get us into that whole area of trying to determine who is at fault in the marriage. Many people spend much time and energy asking the question: is the cause of this divorce legitimate, and does it meet the criteria these exemptions suggest? Dealing with these issues has kept many church leaders busy for a lifetime.

Jesus, in the Gospel of Mark, doesn't give any exemptions. When asked to make a judgment on divorce, whether it is lawful or not, Jesus will not do so. Instead he jumps all the way back to Genesis 1 and 2, to those marvelous verses we examined in the previous chapter.

Here Jesus reasserts in a most powerful way the divine intention for marriage. He rejects the Old Testament approach as being too casual and too insensitive to violations that are taking place in the lives of people. Some husbands are demanding divorce for the most trivial and superficial of reasons. Women are almost powerless. Jesus sees a cruel injustice here, and he wants to put a stop to divorce on a whim.

He unequivocally states that divorce is not in accordance with the intention of God. All of the exemptions that are given here and elsewhere are missing the real point — marriage is meant to last until death do us part. Divorce, according to Jesus, is adultery, it is unfaithfulness to the covenant that has been made between two people. Divorce is a violation of the deep bonding that we have had with another person.

In jumping back over the words of Moses to Genesis 1 and 2, Jesus makes the strongest statement possible about male and female together, about the covenant we have with each other, as equal partners. Harmony is the goal of that relationship. Divorce does not belong to the good of creation. It is not the intention of God for any of us. To try to squeeze out some

## THE NEW TESTAMENT AND DIVORCE

justification from some exemption clause is beside the point. Divorce is wrong. Period.

Then what shall we do with divorce? The most obvious difficulty we have in the New Testament is not with what Jesus said but with what he did not say. In the passage from Mark 10 we have here a very specific situation. If a couple divorces and then the wife remarries, what does this do to the second husband? That is the issue addressed here, but there are many other issues which are not discussed.

For instance, what about the status of a divorced woman if she did not remarry? Was it possible for a single woman to live without the support and protection of a husbnd in those days? What about the first husband? Was he free to marry a woman who had not already been married? There are many questions here that are not addressed. Any attempt to take these words from Mark and make a complete determination of the legitimacy of divorce is just not possible.

Once again we need to look at the whole of Jesus' teaching. What we find so prevalent in the four Gospels is that Jesus is trying above all to portray to us the ideal. He wants to paint a picture of the kingdom of God. He wants to hold up for all to see the divine intention of God for his creation. He was well aware of human sinfulness and failure but nevertheless wanted to challenge all people with the highest, the best, the pure, the ideal. He knew we would not be able to be perfect, yet he wanted to show us the ideal.

The Sermon on the Mount in Matthew 5–7 is a good example of many absolute demands given here. Be perfct as your heavenly father is perfect. Do not resist one who is evil. Love your enemies and pray for those who persecute you. Do not lay up for yourselves treasures on earth where moth and rust consume and where thieves break in and steal. Do not be anxious about your life, what you shall eat or drink or wear. Do not be anxious about tomorrow. Judge not. Don't notice the speck in your brother's eye. And in like manner, do not be divorced.

All of these belong to the ideal of the kingdom of God. This is the way it was meant to be. Jesus is saying to us, look up and see the glorious purpose for which God has created you, to live in complete harmony with God and his will. This is the ideal for all of us, and the ideal is never compromised. At the same time, Jesus is fully aware that none of us can ever achieve that ideal. That is why there was a cross.

Just to make sure that we do not misunderstand the ideal nature of this intention, Jesus uses all sorts of overstatements. We may resist the idea that Jesus would use overstatements, but I don't think we can come to any other conclusion.

For example, "If anyone wants to be my disciple and does not hate his own father and mother and brothers and sisters and even himself, he cannot be one." "If your right hand causes you to sin, cut it off and throw it away." "Do not resist evil." "It is easier for a camel to go through the eye of a needle than for a rich man to enter the kingdom of God." These statements are not to be seen as absolutes to be taken literally. Jesus is describing the ideal, and he knows full well that we will not be able to fulfill that ideal.

To make very sure that none of us falls into the trap of trying to be perfect, to try to be all the ideal says we should be, Jesus redefines the law of the Old Testament: "You have heard it said, do not murder. But I say to you, anyone who is angry with his brother will be subject to judgment. You have heard it said, do not commit adultery, but I say to you, anyone who looks at a woman lustfully has already committed adultery with her in his heart. You have heard it said, love your neighbor and hate your enemy, but I say to you, love your enemies and pray for those who persecute you." In others words, Jesus holds up the ideal, but the ideal is impossible for any one of us. We can never live up to the ideal — not that we should

# THE NEW TESTAMENT AND DIVORCE

not try, but that as human beings we are unable to be what God intended us to be.

At the same time, we must always remember that Jesus was adamantly opposed to any kind of absolute law. He opposed legalism at every point. The kingdom of God, he said, is not a new law, it is grace. The kingdom is not more rules and regulations; it is a relationship with a loving Father. In fact, Jesus made the point emphatically clear when he went and deliberately broke some of the laws, such as eating on the Sabbath. He wanted to make a statement that whenever a law becomes inhumane, whenever it is used to oppress or injure or destroy a precious person, then the law must be disobeyed.

The basic teaching of Jesus and the New Testament is that we are saved by grace through faith. We do not become God's children by following the law or the laws but by God's love in Jesus Christ. In fact, the Gospel is meant primarily for those who know they cannot follow the law, those who go through life messing up time and again. The Gospel is meant for those who fail, those who hate and steal and commit adultery and divorce and love money and all that. Only the sick have need of a physician, not those who are well.

Jesus' response to the woman caught in adultery is instructive. In John 8:4, the people bring a woman to Jesus with the words, "'Teacher, this woman has been caught in the act of adultery. Now in the law Moses commanded us to stone such. What do you say about her?' This they said to test him, that they might have some charge to bring against him.

"Jesus bent down and wrote with his finger on the ground. And as they continued to ask him, he stood up and said to them. 'Let him who is without sin among you be the first to throw a stone at her.' And once more he bent down and wrote with his finger on the ground. But when they heard it, they went away, one by one, beginning with the eldest, and Jesus was left alone with the woman standing before him. Jesus looked up and said to her, 'Woman, where are they? Has no one condemned you?' She said, 'No one, Lord.' And Jesus said, 'Neither do I condemn you; go, and do not sin again.'"

Jesus' answer to those who were hurt, those whose lives had hit bottom was this, "Let those who are without sin cast the first stone." The marriage which is described in Genesis 1 and 2 is the ideal, God's magnificent ideal. But when we cannot fulfill these ideals, when our lives do not measure up, the message is very clear. "Neither do I condemn you." He continues to hold up the ideal at all times, "Do not sin again," knowing that she cannot possibly carry this out. It is at this point where we hear the magnificent words about forgiveness, about seventy times seven, and it is when we see the cross.

In essence, Jesus does not sanction divorce. He holds up as high as he can the wonderful ideal of marriage. At the same time, he does not condemn the person who is divorced but offers unconditional forgiveness and love. He gives us an opportunity to start over again. Jesus avoids the discussion of that day on when divorce is lawful and when it is not. That is never the major issue. Rather, what is important is what has happened in the lives of persons whom Jesus loves. For persons who have been hurt and bruised, Jesus offers love and forgiveness and salvation and wholeness.

For a brief moment, we should also look at what the Apostle Paul has to say. Paul has been accused by all sorts of people for being less than helpful in his words about divorce and in his treatment of women. This is not entirely fair, and I think it would be most accurate to say that much of what Paul most likely said about divorce is simply not recorded. There are really only a handful of verses that deal with divorce, and with divorce such a significant issue in the early church, he must have said a good deal more.

Repeating what was said earlier, Paul responds to the reality of divorce in the early church by adding an exemption clause. There is no valid reason for divorce, he implies, except when one of the partners is an unbeliever. At the same time

## THE NEW TESTAMENT AND DIVORCE

he hoped to slam the door good and tight, he opened it wide. Most people going through a divorce do not seem to have many good things to say about the faith and life of the one to whom they have been married. It would not take much to convince oneself and others that the partner is an unbeliever, and thus divorce is justified.

Thus, as we might expect, Paul's injunction created all sorts of practical problems in the early church. Who is a believer and who is an unbeliever? What is unfaithfulness and what is not? Who is capable of making judgments? Who is innocent and who is guilty? What a quicksand this becomes as we become mired in trying to define what is legitimate and what is not. We will do some of this even today, trying to find a guilty party and an innocent party.

Much of this is beside the point. Divorce is against the ideal of God no matter who might be at fault. In most situations, both partners have significantly contributed to the brokenness that is present. The search for the guilty party, or the attempt to find scriptural defense of a divorce, is usually a misplaced exercise.

One other word about Paul might be helpful. It is clear that he believed the end of the world was very near. Jesus would be returning any moment, maybe even the day after tomorrow. Therefore, Paul basically wants to preserve the status quo. To those who were married and whose marriages might have become unlivable, Paul says to hang in there for just a little longer, for the end is near. For all who are single, it is best that you just stay that way, for all is coming to an end. It is no use to get all hung up on these issues because God is coming again. Paul does not deal with very many of the complexities of marriage and divorce because he believed that more important issues were at stake.

Where he does give some attention to the problems of the people, Paul is also holding up the ideal. He consistently challenges people to become what God intended them to be.

At the same time, he is well aware that we humans never achieve the ideal. "I do not understand my own actions," Paul writes, "for I do not do what I want, but I do the very thing that I hate" (Romans 7:15). That is why he continually proclaims the forgiveness and unconditional love of God in Jesus Christ. "While we were yet sinners, Christ died for us" (Romans 5:8). Nothing in all the world can separate us from the love of Christ — not sin, not divorce, not tragedy, not even death.

A story from today might say it best. There was a pastor who moved to a large congregation in the state of Texas. In reading through the constitution of the church, he discovered that no one who had been divorced was allowed to serve in any leadership positions. He was most surprised and dismayed to see this because he himself had come from a home which had been broken. He knew the pain his parents and he had experienced and wondered why the church was attempting to inflict even more punishment on persons who had already known far more than their share of hurt.

He met with the leadership and raised the question of the constitution. "I see," he said, "that the by-laws of this congregation state that no divorced person can serve in any position of leadership. That is a very interesting statement to me, and I was wondering if you would tell me how this came to be? Why did you decide to prohibit divorced persons from serving as leaders of this congregation?"

"Well," said the leaders, "it is very clear in the Bible. We want to follow the Bible, and this is what it says. Look at the words in I Timothy 3:2-7." So they read together. "Now an overseer (leader) must be above reproach, married only once, temperate, sensible, dignified, hospitable, an apt teacher, no drunkard, not violent, but gentle, not quarrelsome, and no lover of money.

"He must manage his household well, keeping his children submissive and respectful in every way, for if a man does not know how to manage his own household, how can he care

# THE NEW TESTAMENT AND DIVORCE

for God's church? He must not be a recent convert, or he may be puffed up with conceit and fall into the condemnation of the devil, moreover he must be well thought of by outsiders, or he may fall into reproach and the snare of the devil."

The new pastor said to the leaders, "Let's take a closer look at these verses. It says that a leader should be above reproach. I wonder if we all qualify." Some of them hung their heads. "Temperate. I wonder if all of us are temperate. Sensible, dignified, hospitable. Do we fulfill this admonition? Gentle, not quarrelsome. Anyone here that can lay claim to this?

"No lover of money. Is there anyone among us that loves money? Manage your own household well. Can all of you stand up to this? Do you keep your children submissive and respectful in every way? Does this describe your home?"

As the pastor concluded looking at this list from I Timothy 3, he finally summarized that the only ideal included in the prohibition was the one on divorce. All of the rest were conveniently overlooked. In effect, divorce had become the unforgivable sin. Finally the pastor said to the leadership of that church, "You are really not following the Scriptures at all, but you have manipulated the Bible to victimize a group of persons who are already battered." He even used a word like "hypocritical" to describe the actions of the church.

This is often what the church has done. It has taken the tragedy of divorce and made this the unforgivable sin, the eternal mark on the forehead. At the same time it has merely winked at so much else which is against the intentions of God. It is time that we be consistent. Divorced persons have suffered enough. For the church to misuse the Old or New Testament to further clobber them is a violation of the Gospel. These actions ignore the spirit of Jesus and misunderstand the meaning of forgiveness. We can no longer do this.

CHAPTER SIX

# Under the Influence of Chemicals

*D*ENIAL IS ONE OF THE DOMINANT characteristics of our society. We deny what we do not want to accept or believe. If we want the positive badly enough, we somehow will try to deny the negative. We have already examined this phenomenon in an earlier chapter on grief. Denial is often central to that experience. Unfortunately, this denial is much more widespread than we might imagine. It permeates many areas of our lives and serves as a strong deterrent to our becoming whole and well.

By way of example we might look at the tobacco companies in America. All available evidence today from the medical community points to the conclusion that smoking is harmful to our health. There seems to be no question in the minds of most authorities that the use of tobacco is at the root of much serious illness.

Yet the giant tobacco companies who live by the bottom line continue to issue denials. They distribute regular reports

## UNDER THE INFLUENCE OF CHEMICALS

that claim there is no conclusive proof that smoking has any adverse effect. They claim that they are as interested in the public health as anyone else in the country, and if there would be proof of the linkage between smoking and disease, they would indeed get out of the business. Some of the absurdity of the debate was evidenced at a recent Southern Baptist conference. The body as a whole passed a resolution stating that smoking was destructive to the body and therefore against the intentions of God. However, a group of congregations from tobacco growing areas rejected the report and denied there was any evidence to support these conclusions.

All of these denials seem incredible to most of the people in our world, even to many who are smokers, for the evidence of the harmful effects of smoking seems to be beyond question. But denial is a tremendously powerful reality in us, especially if the issue is very close to us. It seems at times that if we do not want something to be true, or if we just cannot let it be so, then somehow we convince ourselves that it is not true. That is denial.

The most serious denial that is present in our society today is in the area of chemical abuse. It is estimated at the present time that one in ten persons is alcoholic, someone who has crossed over that intangible, unmarked threshold, and now is dependent on a chemical. This means that some twenty million Americans are under the influence, with their lives and families being interrupted and affected by this abuse. It seems that in almost every extended family there are one or more persons who are sick with this disease.

When we talk about marriage and divorce, the impact of chemical abuse is staggering. One counselor friend suggests that close to 75% of all couples who come for marriage counseling are dealing with some kind of chemical problem. A national statistic suggests that one out of every two marriages which are in trouble is under the influence, and that one out of every four children in the public schools comes from a family where there is a dependency. We can quote statistics forever in the area of chemical abuse, but it is clear that no mattter what the exact numbers might be, this is a very serious matter.

So often in marriage counseling we deal with all of the other issues. Many sessions are spent discussing in-laws, money, sex, and lack of communication, but somehow things just don't seem to be getting better. The couple often blames the counselor for inadequate help, and the counselor blames the couple for not seriously working on the problem. But just beneath the surface, undetected or unadmitted by those involved, there is the disease called alcoholism. Denial is rampant. Unless this illness is seriously addressed, and unless certain steps are taken to deal with the problem, this marriage is not going to get well.

Much of our denial, much of our unwillingness to address the problem comes from our confusion and ambivalence toward the use of alcohol in our society. Rev. Philip Hansen in his book, *The Afflicted and the Affected*, suggests that when you mention alcohol in our society people either get mad or get thirsty. We really do not know what to do or say about alcohol.

The religious community is equally confused. Some churches give permission for chemical use, while others are caught up in a strongly condemning mode. Neither of these approaches is particularly helpful, especially when the illness of chemical dependency is involved.

One of the most obvious evidences of our denial and ambivalence is found in much of the literature being written on marriage and divorce. It might be said that the publication of books on divorce is one of our fastest growth industries, and this present book may be just more evidence of that. But in looking rather carefully at a large number of books, I have discovered that there is hardly a word written about alcohol being a problem.

Janet Woititz, in her excellent book, *Marriage on the Rocks*, says that Rutgers University has put together a bibliography

## UNDER THE INFLUENCE OF CHEMICALS

of alcohol education which has 873 references. It is a wonderful list. But of these many references, only 38 deal with the effects of alcohol on the family, and the majority of these are pamphlets circulated by Al-Anon groups.

I personally have been most dismayed by this denial, by the absence of help for divorced persons in this area. Even though it is abundantly clear to just about anyone who walks closely with people going through divorce that the illness of alcoholism is very prevalent, most books written about divorce never mention it. There is a very conspicuous conspiracy of silence, and for what reason I am not absolutely sure. Perhaps it is like yelling "fire" in a crowded theater. Most people really do not want to hear about the problems of alcohol. We left that behind a long time ago. Any talk about drinking problems conjures up associations with groups like the Mormons or the W.C.T.U. Until we deal with the problem of alcoholism in marriage, until we admit what impact this is having on marriage and divorce, we will not be able to find the healing that is needed. It is time to accept things the way they are, not as we might like to think they are.

In a book about divorce, it is tempting to just let "sleeping dogs lie". After all, the marriage is over, and even if chemical abuse or alcoholism was involved, that is behind us. Why dredge up painful memories of the past if this is a book about starting over?

However, to ignore the reality of the illness would only be to continue the denial. To be divorced does not end the problem. To be living apart from the alcoholic does not bring about healing either for the spouse or the children. Every person from a dependent family is still afflicted with the illness, even if the family no longer lives together. Unless this illness is treated, it can last for a lifetime. In fact, it can last longer than a lifetime, for this is a sickness that seems to be passed down from generation to generation.

In order to understand this family illness more completely, it is important that we take a look at the effect of the chemical abuse on the alcoholic, on the spouse of the alcoholic, and on the children of the alcoholic. Janet Woititz gives the best analysis that I have found on this subject. Much of the remainder of the chapter will be taken from her writing. I would strongly recommend that her book be read for a more complete study of the effects of chemical abuse.

We begin with some characteristics of alcoholics:

**EXCESSIVE DEPENDENCY.** Alcoholics prefer not to take responsibility for themselves. Rather, they wish someone else to make most of their decisions for them. Drinking does not resolve these dependency problems, but creates even worse dependency. A spouse of an alcoholic often ends up trying to compensate for this irresponsible behavior.

**EMOTIONAL IMMATURITY.** When individuals start drinking alcoholically, they stop developing emotionally. They may look forty years old, but emotionally they are about seventeen. They become just children in the house. And this becomes a constant problem. When alcoholics are busy anesthetizing themselves against unpleasant reality, they cannot develop emotionally. The chronological age and emotional age are different. One indicates an adult and one a child.

**LOW FRUSTRATION TOLERANCE.** Alcoholics have short fuses and no one knows what will set them off. Life itself can ignite the fuse. A spouse and children often get in the way. Alcoholics want things they want when they want them and how they want them! As a result, the rest of the family members often walk around on tiptoe, stepping around any potential conflict. They do not want to trigger the explosion, so they are very, very careful.

**INABILITY TO EXPRESS EMOTIONS.** Alcoholics are often unable to talk about what they are feeling, and they keep these feelings bottled up inside. Emotions are not properly directed and often are not necessarily appropriate to the situation. Feelings are often expressed antagonistically. Alcoholics often dump on others, but the person they are really angry at is the person they see in the mirror each morning. They cannot face the fact of what is happening, so they lash out at others. Things are so mixed up. They may be lying when they think they are telling the truth and telling the truth when they think they are lying. They become strangers when they are drinking; others do not really know them anymore.

**HIGH LEVEL OF ANXIETY IN INTERPERSONAL RELATIONSHIPS.** Alcoholics tend not to make friends easily. They have a feeling of inferiority. There may be drinking friends, but all that really bonds them together are the chemicals. When drinking, an alcoholic can forget the fears and feel in control. Alcoholics are very good at conning others as well as themselves. They promise to give up the booze but cannot give it up. Friendships with other couples fall off as the disease progresses, and they spend less and less time with people who once were close to them. Alcoholics cannot handle closeness. They are too uncomfortable in social situations unless they have been drinking.

**LOW SELF-ESTEEM.** The chemically dependent most often do not see themselves as persons of value. They claim they can handle just about anything. There is no problem that is too big. But then they go and do foolish things, of which they will be reminded by those around them. All of this reinforces those feelings of worthlessness.

**GRANDIOSITY.** Someone has described alcoholics as egomaniacs with inferiority complexes. As they drink they become more and more flamboyant. They become kings or queens as the chemical changes their characters. Alcoholics think nothing of spending money they do not have, for they have a fantasy of making lots of money. "This round is on me." There is no limit to the money alcoholics with grandiose tendencies can spend. They are trying to buy friendship and respect and have nothing else to give. The family then pays the price.

**Feelings of Isolation.** We can love others only to the degree that we love ourselves. Thus, alcoholics are unable to offer and receive love. Love that is given to alcoholics makes them feel guilty. They also feel undeserving, so they retreat to the bottle. People then turn away, and friends no longer want to continue the relationship. Often the family goes the other way when the alcoholic is around. When an alcoholic is truly alone, he or she turns to the only true friend, the bottle. This is such a self-feeding disease. It causes the changes that bring about the excruciating loneliness, and then the sickness offers itself as the only way out.

**Guilt.** Alcoholics are often terribly guilt ridden. They do not want to behave the way they do and do not like themselves when they are drinking. So they promise to stop. This is not a lie; they really mean it. But they do not have a choice, and the disease just gets progressively worse.

## Spouses of Alcoholics

What happens to the spouses of alcoholics? Above all, they should be commended for sheer survival. These people never know what to expect from day to day or hour to hour. They are so often in emotional turmoil. They can't sleep, they don't eat properly, they even look terrible at times. They withdraw from others.

The spouse of the alcoholic often develops a disease that is called "near-alcoholism" which is every bit as damaging as alcoholism. Anyone who has close contact with an alcoholic is affected by the disease, and the spouse is the most vulnerable. No one who is close to an alcoholic escapes responding in at least some of the ways of a near-alcoholic.

The following are some characteristics of the "near-alcoholic":

**Denial.** The spouse denies the disease in many ways. It seems so impossible to believe in the first place, and no one really wants to believe them. Thus the problem is faced in a dishonest manner, or it is not faced at all until life is just overwhelming. Finally, some major threat occurs that cannot be overlooked.

**PROTECTIVENESS.** In the early stage of alcoholism, spouses generally are very understanding. They feel very sorry for their alcoholic mates. They worry about them and try to find solutions to their problems. But this does not help; the alcoholics become more and more skilled at snatching defeat from the jaws of victory. Spouses get sucked in and lose sight of themselves as they try to pacify the alcoholic. They try to make the world right for their mates, to submerge their own needs. More and more they become less and less, but it drains the life right out of them until there is nothing left.

**EMBARRASSMENT.** We care very much about what others think about us, and the behavior of our family members is most important to us. It reflects directly on us. If the alcoholics are behaving outrageously, the spouses are terribly embarrassed. They make excuses and try to become invisible. They don't dare leave the alcoholic with others for fear of more embarrassment. Finally, they try to avoid any situations where embarrassment can occur and stay away from friends and family.

**SHIFT IN RELATIONSHIP.** Near-alcoholic spouses take over and do more and more. They try to become both father and mother to the children, which is impossible. They make virtually all decisions in the house because the alcoholic is another child. Although the near-alcoholic spouses dominate the alcoholics as if they were children, they become very angry and resentful when the alcoholics will not act like adults. The spouses become martyrs, but martyrs are not honored or appreciated much anymore.

**CHANGE OF BEHAVIOR.** After alcoholics have taken over a household, it is not uncommon for the near-alcoholic to become very involved in activities outside of the home — anything to get away. The satisfaction is limited, however, for they are running from, not toward anything. These spouses are not appreciated and respected while at home, but anything that becomes a commitment outside of the home becomes a threat to the alcoholic. Those who are dependent are so needy, so resentful of any energy directed elsewhere.

**GUILT.** Alcoholics are experts at projecting guilt feelings onto their spouses, who become experts in accepting these feelings. When alcoholics accuse their spouses of driving them to drink, the near-alcoholics often take this to heart. They often believe that if they were better spouses, the alcoholics would not drink. The alcoholics agree with this conclusion. When near-alcoholic spouses hear this accusation over a period of time, when they hear how terrible they are, it is almost impossible not to believe it. Much of what they hear is internalized, and they become guilt ridden.

**OBSESSION AND CONTINUAL WORRY.** Life is no longer predictable, and the near-alcoholic spouse is continually worried. What will happen next? Will there be violence? Will my spouse lose a job, walk out on the family, or find another partner? The near-alcoholic spouse may go through the motions of living, but the mind is somewhere else. The more the spouse is involved in the emotional orbit of the alcoholic, the sicker the family becomes. There is the sense of being trapped, control has been lost, and life is a nightmare.

**LYING.** Lying is the way of life in an alcoholic home. The near-alcoholic lies in order to protect the alcoholic. The most destructive of the lies are those that are not meant to be lies, such as when the alcoholic promises to be home at a certain time or carry out a specific responsibility, but does not do so. The alcoholic really means to be honest but is not able to be so. Soon truth loses its meaning, and the spouse doesn't know what to believe, or even what is truth.

**FALSE HOPE AND DISAPPOINTMENT.** The family lives in fantasy, thinking of the alcoholic in terms of what this person could be, not what he or she is. The family is continually disappointed, let down, for this person does not fit its fantasy.

The alcoholic always promises that it will be different. This is accurate. It often is different; it is usually worse. The disease progresses. The alcoholic is in control of the family, which means that all in the family are out of control.

**CONFUSION.** It is hard to think straight. The alcoholic often will have an affair and then complain that the spouse is not understanding. Of course, this is true because no one really understands the alcoholic. When such an affair happens, a spouse is often devastated even though the affair is clearly part of the illness. The spouses are having doubts about self worth in the first place. But now they are not just bad spouses, bad parents, bad persons; now they have lost their sexuality.

**HOPELESSNESS.** No matter what the near-alcoholics do, no matter how hard they might try, it just is not enough. They give and give as if the well has no bottom, but finally they give up. They are physically and mentally exhausted, carrying the whole world on their shoulders. They just cannot do it anymore. They lose interest in everything, and they are truly alone.

## CHILDREN OF ALCOHOLICS

What happens to children? They are just as vulnerable as the adults, if not more so. Children are powerless; they are truly victims of the disease. They are dependent and defenseless. They know no other way of life. Their fathers and mothers are the most important people in their worlds, and if that relationship is sick, the children also are sick.

Some characteristics of children of alcoholics include the following:

**CONFUSION.** The smoke never completely clears, and soon children imitate their parents. This is one of the ways that children learn who they are — by imitation. If parents are unclear, then the children will be unclear. The alcoholic parent is very often one who wallows in broken promises, so the children never know what to believe. It is so confusing, for at times the alcoholic parent is an ideal parent, but when the drinking starts, then the parent is just the opposite.

A daughter can become confused when the father is an alcoholic. She may think of a man as one who drinks. Thus daughters of alcoholic fathers are much more likely to marry active or potential alcoholics. They don't do this on purpose, but unconsciously many girls marry their "fathers".

**LACK OF TRUST.** It is extremely difficult for such children to know what to believe or whom to trust. These children want to believe in the parents but are unable to do so. Boys in an alcoholic family often have trouble seeing themselves as adult males. They simply do not know who they are. A very high percentage of alcoholics come from homes where one or more parents also were dependent. Somehow the sins of the parents are passed on to the children.

**REBELLION.** Children also often rebel against the near-alcoholic spouse. This is the spouse who shields the alcoholic, who has to spin out the many half truths, and who loses all respect of the kids. This is the spouse who usually ends up with most of the discipline and is the safest parent with whom the children can be angry. Children cling to the near-alcoholic for security and yet often reserve much of their anger toward this parent. In fact, when a separation takes place between the parents, children will often choose to go to live with the alcoholic. It is another example of the sickness of such a family system.

**LOW SELF-ESTEEM.** Children of alcoholic homes have often lost a sense of truth. It is not as important to them because it was not important in their homes. These children have had very few consistently supportive experiences in their lives, and as a result their self-esteem has been badly damaged. It has to be. The children from alcoholic homes very often do not see themselves as capable. Down deep they believe that if they were truly capable, they could get the parent to stop drinking.

Thus the children have very mixed emotions. They are unhappy at home, yet they feel needed. They are angry at the alcoholic parent, yet somehow feel responsible. They hunger for the love of both parents, yet feel as if they are pushed away. They feel guilty, yet cannot let go of the feeling that something is wrong with them.

**WITHDRAWAL.** Finally, the social relationships of the children often suffer, for children just do not want to bring anyone home into such a mess. They often withdraw so that they do not have to face others or act in ways that will get others to reject them. It is all just too painful to deal with. There are feelings of aloneness and a lack of self worth. School performance and attitudes suffer as well, and it is hard to imagine how anyone could concentrate on schoolwork when worried about what is going on at home.

## WHAT CAN BE DONE?

What can a loved one of an alcoholic do to find healing and wholeness? What can a spouse or child of an alcoholic do to overcome the trauma and pain of the past and present? How can those who are now separated from the alcoholic find new life and hope? As was mentioned before, it is not enough just to separate or divorce the chemically dependent person. This by itself does not bring wellness. There must be a very conscious effort to find the resources to start over.

The most effective resource for people who have been living with an alcoholic is Al-Anon. Al-Anon is an organization of men and women whose lives have been disturbed and affected by compulsive drinking of others. The organization offers a personal re-orientation process based on the twelve steps of Alcoholics Anonymous. Groups are found almost anywhere in the country and are led by persons who have gone through the same kind of experience in their own lives.

Al-Anon groups meet to discuss the problems and pain created by alcoholism. Group therapy helps all who are present to find peace of mind and to build self-confidence. Everyone in the group has suffered with the same basic struggle and sickness, although it takes many different forms, and will understand what others are saying. There is a strong sense of identification in the group, a spirit of compassion and caring. By participation in Al-Anon a great burden is lifted. Loved ones of alcoholics find they are not alone. God, who deeply cares for people, is very much at work in the healing power and spiritual program of Al-Anon.

There is a strong commitment in Al-Anon to put the illness behind and to begin to live in the present. It is time to let go of all that which is destructive: guilt, fear, hopelessness, denial. It is necessary for near-alcoholics to realize that they did not cause the illness, nor can they cure it. And it is vital to learn the prayer: "God grant me the serenity to accept the things I cannot change, the courage to change the things I can and the wisdom to know the difference."

It is also valuable to attend other support groups. Churches, counseling centers, schools, hospitals, and other institutions often have such groups which can give encouragement and strength.

Those affected by an alcoholic need to find those resources which bring healing. It is now time to move on with life. One suggestion is that those who wish to find healing should put together a list of ten priorities that will be the focus of the future, and then should try to accomplish one of these every day. By doing this, they will learn how to do something which brings confidence and hope.

The overriding purpose of the near-alcoholic is to get healthy. Once help is found, healing pours over the wounds and hurt, then starting over single has great possibilities. Without new health, chances are that the same mistakes will take place all over again. Many near-alcoholic spouses just trade off one alcoholic for another. Following the twelve steps that are found in chapter 10 of this book is one of the best ways to discover this healing. Let go and let God.

Children also should be encouraged to become a part

of Alateen. Alateen is an organization for the children of the alcoholics and has many of the same dynamics which make Al-Anon so effective. Talking to other children who have the same problems is one of the best ways for the children to find resources of healing. The children need to learn much more about the disease and how to detach from it. Their understanding the reality of the situation is the first step in turning themselves around. They will get better as soon as they no longer feel the weight of the burden as theirs alone.

Confusion in the home, which has been the norm, must be changed. Consistency must prevail. This can be accomplished quite easily. There should be specific times for dinner, for homework and for bedtime. The parent should set times and limits and then stick to them. Children should have responsibilities in the home which gives them more security. They then know the parameters of their world and that people do indeed care about them.

The underlying basis for all of this is love. There is no way to give children too much genuine love. It is important that children are told how much they are loved, that they be held close. This will not smother them or spoil them but will give them security. The spouse of the alcoholic should avoid giving unearned privileges to the children or buying them things to overcompensate for the alcohol.

The greatest gift for children and adults is love. Just as God has given this love to us, so we can share it with our children. "I love you because you are you." We communicate to our children that they do not have to earn this love, and they do not risk losing it. Just as God's parental love is self-giving, sacrificial, and unconditional, so parents also need to model this for their children. Only love can ultimately help the child find healing from the effects of having an alcoholic parent.

## CHAPTER SEVEN

# Bringing Myself into Focus

*Talk by Rev. Janet Tidemann,
Starting Over Single Seminar*

My Name Is Janet Ryan Tidemann, and I am a pastor at St. James Lutheran Church. My name is telling in a way. I used to be Janet Ellen Ryan, and I really liked my name. Then I married and became Janet Ellen Bosch, then I divorced and I became Janet Ryan Bosch, and then I married again and I became Janet Ryan Tidemann.

Not too long ago I received a letter from the bank addressed to Ms. Janet Ellen Ryan Bosch Tidemann, on two lines. The lady who wrote to me began the letter with the words, "Dear Janet Ellen".

We go through a lot of changes. For women, a name change often accompanies that identity change. Men usually get to keep their name, so they go through their identity changes under cover. If we have gone through a divorce, we have gone through a lot of changes.

I would like to center on the theme of "Bringing Myself into Focus". I chose that phrase because I do believe we go

## BRINGING MYSELF INTO FOCUS

through a time of trying to figure out who we are or what we are and how we are going to fit into life, when our roles and our patterns and our places have changed.

We are bringing ourselves into focus all of our lives, from the day we are born until the day we die. We are always adjusting and re-adjusting and viewing ourselves in terms of inner needs and other people's expectations. In fact, much of the time in bringing ourselves into focus, we take our cues from other people. We take up roles that are easy to perform, because we have learned them from our moms and dads, from other people, and from society.

If the pressure isn't very great and life is rolling along, it is easy to play house, or play mom and dad, falling into roles that are predetermined in many ways. Often we consent readily to being what other people expect us to be.

However, when we come into a situation of conflict, and we are forced to decide who we are or what we are going to be, then it is hard. This bringing into focus can be painful, it can be confusing, it can be frightening. It can also be very wonderful.

When we first marry, I did this when I first married, we build what I call "stone houses". We tend to adopt a way to behave and a way to relate to other people. Other people invite us to be something and we say, "Okay, we can be that." We build for ourselves a solid, sometimes restrictive, expectable kind of life, and it is like a stone house. It is rigid and easily recognizable. We can go back to it over and over, and people know just what to expect from us.

That stone house is what we are for everyone else, the role that we play. It is the life habits, the patterns and routines that we live. Some people live there all of their lives. They live life in a way that is determined by those around them and never do much self exploration.

As long as we don't grow, or get any bigger in our self expression or in our experience of life, as long as we don't flail around too much, or try to move much, or try other ways of living, that stone house suffices just fine.

When it comes to a disruption, such as divorce, then the conflict and change and explosiveness that occur break up that stone house and fling us out into the world. It is this kind of breaking up that is very painful, and we find ourselves adrift.

We don't know where the walls are, we don't know where the windows are, we don't know where the limits are. We may not have a routine that we recognize or need to have anymore. We may not have any limits. We can stay out until three every night, except that it is very hard on the job. We could eat hot fudge sundaes three times a day, but that is hard on the wardrobe. We are flung out of those patterned ways of living, and we feel lost.

We go from what was once a kind of frozen image to a rather terrific blur as far as self-identity is concerned. We get confused and scared, curious and resentful, and all kinds of things. We must go from day to day as we always did but without the expectations we once had. We are now forced to move from that life to this one.

We all find ourselves in our own private wilderness. That wilderness can be like trying to forge your way through the bush, or like finding your way through a city you have never seen, or like being in a desert or climbing a mountain.

It can also be a place where you find some "life-giving water", sometimes where you find some beautiful and unexpected things. But that wilderness, if we are going to come into being on our own terms, is something all of us have to go through. We have to identify it and face it. Often we find ourselves right in it before we realize we are there. We have to move through it in order to come out on the other side.

Of course, the "living water" is a bonus, and I am sure that all of you have already discovered something of that in your own pilgrimage. "Living water" are words that I get from the book of John when Jesus says, "I will be living water for you".

The "living water" can be a counselor, a friend, an art form, a self discovery. There are so many ways in which the Spirit is moving with us and in us that can be the "living water" in our wilderness. We are given, in this terrible experience of being thrust into life on our own, a real chance to discover who and what we are in a way that most married persons probably never do. They don't have to do it, and probably when we were married, we never did it either. Life was easier from day to day if we did not push into the wilderness or even stick our toes into it.

It is only when we have to that we muster up the courage to bite the bullet, swallow the pride, and fall on our faces, and follow the leading of the Spirit, which was always there but never listened to before. We find ourselves coming into being at the hands of the world and God all at the same time. It is both painful and life-giving.

I would like to share with you my own journey. I realize that everyone's journey is different, so I don't expect that you will identify altogether with me. I hope that you will find some touch points for yourself, some common experiences that help you feel not so alone, not quite so scared or mystified, not quite so guilty; for all of us walk around with a lot of guilt.

Maybe you will find some points which make it possible for you to say, "It was not that way with me at all." In any case, hearing one person's story helps us bring our own into clearer focus. It will give you a chance to make some different interpretations of your own experience and help you find some different ways to look at what has happened to you.

## My Story

When my husband and I told the children we were going to divorce, they started out by thinking we were going to be exactly the same as we had always been. They ran straight out into the raspberry patch, and they picked raspberries in a fine way — just pick, pick, pick, talk, talk, talk. After they had their huddle, they came into the house and said, "Well, you and dad are doing things just as you have always done. You always burn the hamburgers in order to get them done faster, and he always buys the first thing he sees in the store."

They felt we were in a terrible hurry and weren't considering things well enough. However, a year later I got a birthday card from my kids, and they were really good at picking something just right for mom. This birthday card said, "Wishing whatever it takes to make your day." They didn't know what was going on, but they felt things were changing.

I asked my daughter, who is now 17, how she thought I had changed since our divorce. "Well", she said, "it seems like you got taller and your hair turned gray." I was changing and the kids were a little in the dark.

Mine is the familiar story of a girl who had been cherished and loved and always taken care of, who was never prepared for growing up. Upon nearing the end of college, the prospect of finding a job and living on my own was impossible for me even to consider, so I frantically arranged my own marriage in college. I truly believed that everyone in the whole world was already married, already taken, and I was consciously terrified to leave that place unmarried.

I arranged a marriage to a very stable, responsible, good man who could take care of me. I believed that the very minute we were married it would be wonderful, but as we drove down the road after the wedding I looked at those wedding rings and was afraid of what would happen. The me at 20 had just begun to make herself known. She was coming into being but now drew herself into a tight little ball and hid somewhere.

The survivor in me took over, pretending to be the strong woman I thought my mother always was. I became a dutiful wife and a conscientious mother. I was a contributing member of society and tried very hard to be a good person. I suppose

I succeeded as well as the next person.

I am really an undercover poet. When I am in the depths of despair or in wild frustration or cannot sleep because I am so passionately angry or upset, I write poetry. Writing helps me wring things out of myself and get them in front, so I can look at them. It also makes a good record — something like having a journal. I am not an expert poet, but I hope you can share the experiences in my poems.

You can either laugh at or identify with the first poem. It is the way I looked at my preparation for marriage and for life as a female. It has to do with sexual preparation, but it is really much broader than that.

### THE FASTIDIOUS VESTIGIAL VIRGIN

*Sweet little girl with springy curls,*
*Pigeon toes and teeth like pearls*
*Tease your daddy, please your mom,*
*Be a princess at the prom.*

*Be seductive, clever, coy,*
*But save yourself for the golden boy.*

*Fall in love, exhibit passion,*
*Offer up a tempting ration*
*Of halting touches, revealing dresses,*
*But dutifully interrupt caresses.*

*You may know many young men yet,*
*But Mother cautions, "Never pet!"*

*They'll use you, leave you, and tell a friend.*
*And you may come to a single end.*
*Mister Right is somewhere waiting —*
*So just keep up your anxious dating.*

*Sure enough, he does appear,*
*And as the wedding day draws near*
*She waits with delicious, quivering fright*
*For that long prepared for wedding night.*

*But, alas, when asked to deliver,*
*All she can muster is a shiver.*
*For after years of hearing sex knocked,*
*She just can't get her knees unlocked.*

This attitude of mine probably contributed to a lot of our lack of communication. As time went on, I changed, and I began to feel as if I didn't know who I was at all. I was really a good mom, and I could cook, and I could make curtains, and I could entertain. I could do a lot of things that looked pretty good, and so in the middle of that time I wrote a poem about a cookie.

Interestingly enough, at Christmas one year I sent out a mimeographed sheet and on it was the Virgin poem, the Cookie poem, and a recipe for pumpkin bars. When I look back now it was just a horrible mess of not knowing who I was.

### COOKIE

*Squeezed as from a cookie press*
*I view myself with some distress,*
*An object liked, but not admired,*
*Considered sweet, but not inspired;*
*Providing pleasure, not nutrition,*
*Meant for decoration, not ambition.*

*A cookie is made to be pretty and sweet,*
*Even more prized if clever and neat —*

*But my picture of me has suddenly come*
*Full circle from cookie*
*To shapeless Crumb.*

As life became more and more unlivable at home, I became deeply interested in God, in studying, in theology, and I wanted to make intimate friends. These were means of taking me outside the house. My life became more and more unsettled. I had a strong sense of myself as terribly ugly, misshapen, and not allowed to come into being.

I must also say that my former husband also had a very painful, frustrated personal story that is valid. In all my defining of myself and working things out, very little of it had anything to do with him. He was in prison too, and he didn't know what to do either. Both of us suffered a lot of pain. We were mutually helpless, unprepared for being grown up together. The way we lived together was that he was definitely the parent and I was the child, and I did not know how to grow up.

### The Couple

*Ugly girl-child, stooped,*
    *eyes down, hunching along*
    *the wall*
    *she is large for her age.*

*Fed and cared for*
    *urged toward domestication*
    *but she is wild*
    *and will not sit demure*
    *upon the loveseat*
    *sipping coffee with the rest.*

*Something would snap in her*
    *and send the pieces flying*
        *into oblivion.*

*The Princess cannot show her face.*

> *The keeper is a handsome prince*
> *straight and dark and tall*
> *good beyond the telling*
> *there is nothing he can't do — or won't*
> *to make the beast's life better.*
>
> *He gives her things*
> *and lets her have her freedom*
> *In manageable degrees.*
>
> *He seems to be kindly disposed toward her*
> *and beds her regularly*
> *and it is this she cannot understand*
> *creature that she is.*
>
> *The Princess must not show her face.*
>
> *Secret, told, would one bright flame*
> *fly up, then gutter into ashes.*
> *Held, would feeble, die*
> *for lack of air.*
> *What choice but tell in dreaming;*
> *feed in fevered fantasy?*
> *Prisoner secret,*
> *will you not become grotesque*
> *before your warder's eyes?*

At this point I was fighting for my life. I realized after my divorce that my children also had been fighting for their lives. They were very easy, sweet, obedient children. My son was a parent pleaser kind of kid; he studied well. My husband and I did a good job of parenting together. At 17 our son had never dated, never had a job. The most he did was to play poker with some other boys his age. He stayed in his room and studied very hard.

My daughter lived in her bedroom for four years. She only came out for meals and could hardly stay at the table. She saved up money and bought a color TV which made her bedroom even more livable, and she stayed in there with the cat. The cat, her best friend, thought that my daughter was her mother. The cat was very snooty toward anyone else; she would always run and hide.

The day that we separated my son went looking for job. Within two weeks he had a girlfriend. That isn't necessarily good, but he seemed as if he had been afraid to live before that, to get on with things. The day my former husband moved out, my daughter picked up the TV and came out of her room. The cat came out also. Within three months the cat was the most friendly, the most bothersome, the most persistent, loving cat you ever saw.

This is not to say that my husband was responsible for the failure of our marriage. But the atmosphere in our home was oppressive. We never fought or argued or said an unkind word, but you could tell something was wrong. Nobody could really live. Now my children have proceeded to get on with their living. Thus, after the divorce our children have changed in some very good ways.

My own self-image changed. One thing that happened to me was traumatic. The first week on my own I had to write the checks for the bills, and I had never done that before. I had been married for 18 years and had never done that! As I sat at the desk I realized that I had never done that either, never sat in the chair at the desk in the living room! I remember clearly that when I sat down at the desk I expected my feet to dangle and swing on the chair, because I felt so little.

But I did get the bills paid. I found it wasn't hard. I just read the bills and those lines on the bottom and then wrote the same numbers on the check. It came out right. I realized that I was terribly anxious about all that. I had a drastically reduced budget, and I had to be very careful about everything that I spent. I found that frugal living is much simpler than moneyed living. I just never went shopping and didn't have to make any decisions.

I remember one very bad experience that was quite emotional for me. My son had had his high school senior pictures taken, and I had agreed to pay for them. I went to the bank and deposited my money, then went to the photography studio and paid for the pictures by check. Three days later I found that because it was after 3 p.m. the bank had not honored my deposit, but the bank surely had honored the photographer's cashing my check at 4:30 p.m.! So I was overdrawn and it cost me six dollars. That amount was just like a fortune! I remember sitting and crying, outraged at my helplessness. I never have forgotten this, and thus think of young householders who must sit and do this kind of counting every month. How frightening that was, and is!

I went up and down. I did some things I really enjoyed, and I was feeling better. Then my friend Nancy had her 40th birthday party. I was very excited to go and share it with her. She held a big open house in the middle of the afternoon. I got all spiffed up and told my kids I was going to Nancy's party. I drove over there, got out of the car, walked in, and then thought to myself, "I am either going to faint or throw up." I didn't know which, but I had to leave. I told Nancy that I had to leave, that I would call her later, and I left.

It was an experience of sheer terror, because I didn't know who I was! What if people would ask me where my other half was. If I would have had to explain, I would have been overcome with a mindless terror. When I came home that afternoon, my children thought I had forgotten something, but I told them I just couldn't go. That didn't happen to me again, but it was a terrible thing. I am sure that many others have gone through that as well. I thought this must be how people feel who can't go out ever, who have that kind of fear.

I began to realize that I had lived inside of the house for eighteen years. I wouldn't go outside. I used to look at beautiful days and think they were for other people and not for me, and I would keep baking and cooking and sweating in the kitchen even if it were summer. But I did not go outside.

One time a counselor said to me, "I think you were an emotional suicide. You kept yourself very closeted and wrapped up. You didn't feel your feelings and your joy and your world." I almost felt a yearning at that time to be some kind of animal, so I wrote a poem.

### LEAVE THE DOOR AJAR

*Leave the door ajar*
*and never mind about the flies;*
*I need to smell the sky.*

*And when I leave*
*there will be no more*
*talking to me then.*
*For I will be*
*the rabbit in the field*
*and your desperate soundings*
*will only make me startle*
*and softly disappear.*

*Leave the door ajar.*
*I need to hear the grass.*

One of the other experiences that I had was in telling people that I had divorced. I am sure all who have been divorced have to tell others about it. I wrote my brother. He had been the classic maverick, in and out of a lot of adventures, and I love him to pieces.

When he received the news, he called me. In 36 years of hearing his voice, I felt I had never really heard his true voice. He was usually full of excitement about something, but this time the person on the phone sounded a lot like my dad. He said to me, "I know what has happened to you, and I have never had a lot to offer, but I will be for you whatever you need, and you can call me anytime." That was a wonderful experience for me, and it was gratefully received.

My dad was very confused by the whole thing. He came and asked me, "Can you tell me, please, what happened?" So we talked about all sorts of things we had never talked about before — we talked about sex and about talking to each other. When we got through my dad said, "Well, it sounds to me like you were probably two very nice people who just never should have been married to each other." I was very, very grateful for those words.

Christmas came, and I sent out a letter to friends. Of course, when people get letters about divorce with their Christmas cards, we should expect to get something back in return, and so I did. From one pastor and his wife I received, "To wish you the joy and hope and the wonder of Christmas... We are so disappointed to hear about you. It is hard to understand, especially in light of your commitment to Christ."

I got a couple more of those letters. I felt as if I were opening letter bombs. Another came from a woman who is known for her counseling skills. "Dear Janet, when I got your letter I got so sick to my stomach that I had to lie down, and I just lay there the whole afternoon, and my tummy just churned and churned."

Another letter came from a single woman who is close to 60 years of age. "I wonder how you feel about all the changes in your life. I love you and wish you happiness, whatever it takes." We all receive the good and the bad.

In the middle of all of this, I began my work as an intern pastor. I had been assigned this internship sometime before; now when I came to the job I was a divorcee, and I was panicky. I didn't know how in the world to present this new information. The pastor said, "We do not need a congregational announcement about this. Some people will know and some people will not. If it comes up, you can say it; if not, don't worry about it."

The very first meeting I went to was a missionary meeting. I sat down next to an 82-year-old lifetime missionary from

China. I said hello to her. She said, "Well now, are you a married lady or a single lady?" I thought, "Oh, don't ask!" So I said, "I am a divorced lady." She said to me, "Well, I will have to have you over for lunch soon. I have been single all of my life." This was a very nice way to start. I found I was projecting all of my own feelings about divorce onto other people. The comments of other people were not as bad as I thought they would be.

Other experiences I had were with friends. I found that sometimes when you are knee-deep in trauma or crisis, other needy people come to you and you don't have anything to give. To be a seminary student at my age was peculiar, to be a divorced student was even stranger, and then to be a woman was absolutely unique. There was one woman who I think believed I would make a good term paper or something. She used to buy my coffee and want to talk and see if I would tell her things. I figured that out and became angry about it. I wrote a poem in one of my angry states.

### THIS BUTTERFLY SPINS A WEB

*She said,*
  *"I'd like to get to know her better."*
*She said,*
  *"I think she could be worth my time."*

*Well, sweetheart,*
  *You can have a pretty dance or two*
  *For what a cup of coffee costs*
  *And the time it takes to drink it*
    *while it's hot.*

*But, mind you —*
 *If you ask admission to my private rooms,*
 *Beware!*
   *The dancing was a ruse,*
   *And easy singing told you nothing at*
     *all.*

 *Under the silver wings*
 *Is one hair shirt —*
   *a second skin*

*Now —*
 *Let the coffee grow cold in the cup.*
 *Descend into the room*
   *where hangs one naked bulb*

 *that shows up one who doesn't dance or sing*
 *but crouches,*
   *crying*
     *"What was I supposed to do?*

     *I wore the dress;*
     *I sang the song.*
     *But no one knew my name..."*

*You!*
 *With the stale coffee.*
 *You thought I'd tell my name,*
   *and maybe even yours into the bargain?*

*Well,*
 *There is no name for me.*

 *And are you still so sure of yours?*

There was another friend whose family was struggling with drug abuse. We had gone to college together and had been very dear friends all those years when our lives were riding along just fine. Now we were there for each other when our lives began falling apart. After spending a lot of time together with my pain and her pain, I wrote the following poem.

### TEETER TOTTER

*You're up, I'm down.*
   *We hesitate*
     *and, achingly aware of each one's place,*
     *elation — devastation,*
   *Two far points on one broad scale,*
*Take strength from being still together.*

*You're down, I'm up,*
   *And as we gauge the changed positions,*
     *softly say, "I understand, you know,*
     *because I've been there, too."*
   *We won't stay here forever, either,*
*My joy won't last — and neither will your grief.*

*We strike an even balance,*
*Hold each other's eyes in expectation,*
*Relish the tension in the moment*
   *So very, very still....*

   *Poised*

     *Craving flight*

*Press the earth*          *And soar*

                 *I AM HERE!*

                   *kno-*
                   *wing*
                  *knowing*
                 *KNOWING*
                 *KNOWING*

*I AM HERE!*

Friends will help us through. Through all of this, church and God and religion in general were all up for grabs. The church had represented forgiveness and goodness and beauty and stability. Suddenly it was the last place where I felt comfortable. It was the last place I wanted to be when I was in the most pain, and it was the last place that seemed to offer me much of anything.

As I look back on it now, part of the reason for my feeling this way was that I was changing so much, and what had been artificial in my life didn't suffice anymore. I needed something else. What I had found sufficient before was failing. I imagined the church as being like an empty sepulchre.

*FAILED*

*Empty, aching empty.*

*Spaces once loud legend filled with*
*    Pageant sounds, cheering, chanting,*
*        Whispers, whispers,*
*Spinning, whirling, swinging round*
*To keep the spaces fully occupied.*

*Now not any story tells me*
*    When the heart should beat, when breathe.*
*Empty — splayed and helpless,*
*    Insides like a burnt out cave*
*        Abandoned.*

*The night wind flies*
*    Sharp icy into me*
*    And howls*
*        Hollow hollow hollow.*

Nothing meant much to me in terms of faith, and this emptiness and loss of God became a nightmare to me. I had never had nightmares before, but now I would wake up screaming in fear, mindless fear. But because of the dreams I found that for the first time I absolutely believed that there was eternal life. I still remember the rush of "yes" feelings as I began to wake up. "Yes, I know there is life after death."

## BRINGING MYSELF INTO FOCUS

From that time on I realized to ask God, if God was anywhere at all, to stay by me, to be with me — not to do anything, not to show me any tricks, not to tell me why, just to be there somehow. I also realized that it had been God somewhere within me for a long, long time that had been prodding me toward life.

Even though I had a lot of pain and dissatisfaction, there was a nagging that wouldn't let me get away with denial or avoidance or superficial living. God was there. Like it or not, God was there. I needed to ask God to stay because it seemed as if nothing else in life was going to be good unless I had some relationship with God.

### CONSTANCY

*Oh, God, who dragged me through the years*
*when I would only cover up my eyes*
*and dig my heels into the ground;*

*Who woke me up each morning after*
*I had tried to kill myself each night*
*with sudden, dreamless sleep;*

*Who whispered, "Teach," "Drink coffee," "Study,"*
*when my desperation turned to running,*
*but my courage only funded stopgap measures;*

*Oh, God, who finally turned me in upon myself*
*to name the desert of my choosing,*
*and point me toward the wilderness*
*that holds out terror and some hope;*

*Oh, God, who takes my eyelids, steals my sleep*
*and confounds me daily, hourly —*

> *Oh, God, won't you please, please*
> *touch my shoulder now and then*
> *as I walk into my pain*
> *and let me hear again the words*
> *that start with "Lo, lo I am with you..."*

With this prayer I began to realize that I was moving forward. Finally I was having a sense of something that I knew was a grounding and that I could ask for that. I was in motion toward. I was leaving things behind and actually seeking and hoping for God to provide some living water. I was finding that God was providing that living water.

Friends and family, new discoveries about myself, and new appreciation of the world were now mine. God had lost all identity for me for awhile, and I needed something back. At that point I was willing to let it all go and start over. So I wrote a poem.

### Answer

*What did you do*
*When you first heard that*
  *God was dead?*

*I'll tell you what I did.*
*I had a good night's sleep*
*And kept the day's sins to myself.*

*And in the morning*
*I went out to greet the sun*
*And ask around to find out*
  *Who it is, then,*
*That puts the dew upon the grass*
*And rabbits in the field*
  *And your hand in mine.*

God is persistent, and if you think God is dead, God will tell you something else.

I think that all of the changes, all of the pain, all of the loving care and friendship, everything that happens to us, become a part of us. From the moment that we start to painfully, consciously, make the struggle to grow, it all helps us to bring ourselves into focus.

It all creates us anew. We are not the same people we were before the struggle started, not the same people we were before the pain, the joy, the new friends. Nor are we the same as before we were in the wilderness or before we found the "living water".

All of this marks us. I think it is important to own the marks, to wear the marks. My hair turned gray, and it feels rather good. I turned forty, and it feels fine. There were many years when I didn't feel good about being my age, but I have come to appreciate everything that has gone into getting me there. We are marked by a lot of things, and I have put them in a poem.

### MARKED

*Marked by a star*
  *She carries borrowed light*
  *And some may find it in her eyes.*

*Marked by a river*
  *Flows her life more*
  *Surely than before.*

*Marked by the wind*
  *She wears a softer dress that*
  *Moves against her skin*
  *And makes her smile.*

*Marked by pain and pleasure, she
  Brings fresh flowers to her face
  And breathes the fragrance
  Of well-tended memories.*

*Marked for change
  She is a woman
  Bearing star and wind and river
  And, just a little breathless,
  Marked growing child of God, forever.*

# CHAPTER EIGHT

# CHILDREN OF DIVORCE

*Talk by Rev. Ted Kalkwarf,*
*Starting Over Single Seminar*

WE AS ADULTS HAVE THE RESPONSIBILITY of helping our chldren understand what they are feeling during the experience of divorce. There is often a rainbow of many different kinds of feelings, and we need to accept the diversity of these feelings. Because most childrn have not encountered the intensity and the longevity of feelings like this before, they often do not understand what is happening to them. They may have much difficulty in expressing these feelings to us or to anyone else.

Often we as adults do not want to confront the pain that our children feel, for their pain brings up the pain that we feel. We would just as soon not open up this area, so often we choose to avoid what our children are experiencing, or we blame ourselves for what the children are feeling.

More than anything else we want our children to stop hurting, to not suffer any of that which we are suffering. Thus we sometimes try to force the children, most of all by subtle means, to stop hurting. We do this by offering too much reassurance, too much protection, and by smothering the emotions of our children. But we cannot protect our children from hurt and pain; we can only help them to express these feelings.

There are not only the children in our lives to be concerned about, but also the child which is in each of us, our "inner child of the past". We never completely outgrow that child within. Dr. Paul Tournier, the famous Swiss psychiatrist and author, explains, "I am 69 years old and my wife just died, and the feelings I have are the same that I had when I was four years old and my mother died."

Tournier said that he wanted to respond to this death of his wife in the same way that he had reacted as a four-year-old boy. In dealing with the feelings of our children, we must also confront the feelings that are from that child "within", with some of the hurts and pains of our own childhood. This often brings up pain or grief we would rather forget, and it means that our conversations with ourselves or with our children can get rather sticky.

To truly help our children, we need to keep them from building up the damaging feelings that are inside of them. It is neither possible nor helpful to try to prevent them from experiencing the full range of painful feelings. The only way to get rid of these feelings is to express them. Buried pain does so much damage. It festers and hurts from deep within the child. To prevent the expression of such hurt feelings is a short-circuiting of the grieving process.

Whatever else divorce might be for a child, it is above all a tremendously significant loss. We can never underestimate this sense of loss, this sense of sadness. Thus it is important that the parents not run away from the pain or try to take away the child's discomfort.

At the same time, we do not want to reverse roles, where the children in a sense become the parents who take care of the adults. It is not fair to children to ask them to give parents that kind of support. To try to understand the children's hurt takes courage, courage to listen to the pain while knowing that the parent's pain might be increased. It may even mean that we take some blame without becoming defensive. When we take time to experience these feelings with our children, we usually find that we too receive comfort.

What are the feelings that a child experiences through divorce? There are specific stages through which children often pass, although the specific order in which these are experienced often differs. Don't expect children to bypass these stages, but pray that going through them will be a positive rather than a negative experience. Much of this will depend on how well parents are able to listen.

## FEAR AND ANXIETY

No matter how open or how hidden the conflict may have been, the announcement of the separation or the actual moving out or the divorce itself is almost always a surprise to the children. The normal emotional reaction to this announcement is one of fear. Suddenly a great unknown has been opened up in front of the children, and they are being pushed into that great unknown.

The separation of the parents is the shaking of everything stable and sure, an earthquake of the highest magnitude. This is due, in part, to children who usually believe that mothers and fathers have no other purpose than to be moms and dads. Parenting is the only role the children understand, especially younger children.

Fear and anxiety have physical as well as emotional responses. Sweating, restlessness, sleeplessness, nightmares, hyperventilation, pain in the chest, gastro-intestinal disturbances and a wide variety of aches and pains often accompany the experience of parents' divorce. It really hurts deep inside for the children of divorce.

Quiet reassurance needs to be given to children, and

we need to discuss our plans with them. This should be done plainly and very clearly. We can all deal with what we know far better than with what we imagine. If our children are not given helpful facts, then they will imagine much worse possibilities. When one parent has left, it is not at all uncommon for children to fantasize that now the other parent will abandon them as well.

This fear and anxiety, this need to know what is taking place, will continue in the life of children for some time, no matter how much we try to make things secure for them. It is always better to say what is going to happen, even if this creates a greater reaction in the beginning. In the long run, a child who knows what is going on will deal better with fear than one who does not know.

It is most important to spend quality time with children during this period. Love the children openly, for love is the greatest antidote to anxiety. I John 4:18 says, "Perfect love casts out fear." But it is often hard to love children when they are feeling rigid, when they would prefer to lie in bed with the covers up over their heads.

It is also difficult when our children do not want to spend time with us, when they shut us out. Sometimes when we are on the outs, when communication is not very good, it is best just to give our children a back rub. In this quiet sense of closeness and touching and compassion, we can communicate our love and understanding more than with words.

## ABANDONMENT AND REJECTION

Children most often feel abandoned by the parent who leaves. One eight-year-old child said, "If my dad really loved me, he would not leave mom and me." It is a highly confusing time for children, and younger children cannot distinguish between parents separating from each other and from them.

These feelings of abandonment can be reduced if the parent who leaves can keep strong contact with the children during these first stages. Unfortunately, this is more easily said than done, for it is at this time when there is often the most conflict or disagreement between the parents. Thus, the temptation is for the parent who leaves to have minimum contact with those still in the home, including the children.

To deal with the feelings of abandonment and rejection, there needs to be an extra effort made at contact, particularly by the parent who has left. Telephone calls will not accomplish this. What children need to overcome the feelings of abandonment is the actual physical presence of the parent.

A teen-age girl complained about a loss of contact this way, "I see my father just one hour a week. I either end up preparing his evening meal for him or going out to dinner with him and his new woman friend. Why can't my dad just spend one hour with me alone?" She was feeling resentment and abandonment. Children need as much structure and personal attention as we can give to bring a sense of security to their upended world.

## ALONENESS AND SADNESS

Children of divorce often feel very much alone. They believe that no one else in the world is experiencing the same emotions and pain that they are. It is a time of aloneness. Regular family activities have come to a halt; mealtimes are often much more irregular. Even the conflict which had been so familiar now is not present in the home.

Children find for the first time in their life a deep feeling of sadness, which takes a significant toll on the normality of life. Hobbies are neglected, pets are ignored, fish bowls aren't cleaned, and the energy of the children is diminished. Many children lose interest in school work, and they may become addicted to television.

Children of divorce often spend a lot of time thinking; some of it usually is wishful thinking. They may fantasize that the parents will reconcile and that all of the problems of the past and present will vanish. Perhaps the children believe that they will be the ones to find a way to make this happen. This only intensifies the sadness, and tears may be commonplace. Spells of crying should not be discouraged, tears are an important outlet. Crying can be a very important psychological function to help us overcome our sadness.

We live in a society where we tend to suppress our painful feelings, but if we felt the freedom to cry more often we would all be more healthy. This is especially true for men and for older boys who have been trained not to cry. Instead we take to ourselves ulcers and heart disease. Now in a world where equal rights for both men and women are a theme, women are also learning how to suppress their pain and are suffering more heart attacks.

## FRUSTRATION AND ANGER

A feeling of frustration is created when children cannot get what they want. In the case of a family, what children want primarily is security and happiness. They want things to be the way they were before the divorce. So they become frustrated, and this frustration often becomes anger. Anger may be directed almost anywhere: at parents, at teachers, at friends, at themselves.

Part of the frustration comes from a sense of powerlessness. Children are unable to change their parents. No amount of anger is going to change the adult behavior. Decisions are being made outside of the children's influence.

When the anger is directed inward, children often do things to hurt themselves. Many adults who go through the Fifth Step of the Alcoholics Anonymous program describe how their own use of chemicals was motivated by their parents' divorce, how they believed that if they became messed up, the parents would have to come back together to deal with them. Both parents together could fix them up. But their own dependency grew so fast they were unable to handle it.

Children's anger should be received naturally. Parents need to share reassurance that it is normal to feel the way they do. We do not blame them for their anger. Children of divorce have a right to their feelings, and one of these feelings can be anger. Let them tell us why they are angry, let them share their frustration, give them the invitation to talk and express feelings. When we can receive the anger, the hurt feelings, without defending or excusing ourselves, a healthy bond is created between us.

## Resentment

Anger often results in a pulling away, creating a distance between the children and the parents. Here the children are trying to protect themselves from further emotional pain, or they may be punishing the parent for what has happened. This may be a double whammy for the parent. There is not another adult in the marriage to give support and strength, and now the children may turn on them as well.

This rejection can also take the form of pouting, of a cold war and a silent treatment. The children dig in their heels; they won't come when called and won't respond when addressed. When asked to carry out some task the children either resist or conveniently forget. Older children become very critical and are constantly complaining about brothers and sisters.

It is a strange time, for when children are going through this resentment, they are pushing the parents away at the very time they want to be held. Or they are saying hateful things when they want most of all for the parents to be loving. In this way the children are protecting themselves from further rejection.

Sometimes the children and the parents can work out a new structure, a new understanding, a new way of relating. But then so often a new adult enters the picture and the parent turns to the new partner for love and affirmation. Now the children will often do things to sabotage this new relationship, for they do not want to be vulnerable to be hurt again. If the children can prevent this new relationship from being formed, this provides a means of protection.

## RE-ESTABLISHED TRUST

This is the goal for which parents and children strive. It is a time of freedom and liberation. The cool breeze has started to blow in an otherwise hot and stuffy room. How long this takes is subject to great variety. Each situation is different. The recovery time depends on the conflict, the age and personality of the children, and how the parents have managed the divorce. It can take a couple of months or a couple of years.

There are five things that parents can do to make sure the children's feelings return to normal as soon as possible:

1. Parents must avoid being preoccupied with only their own feelings. It is so easy to miss the feelings of children, to be insensitive, to be too busy. But parents must make time to listen to these feelings. Certain times of the day should be set aside when parents have sufficient energy to listen to what children want to say. Adults should use their own network of friends for personal support, so that they can have the freedom to give themselves to their children.

2. Parents should allow time for healing. This is not the time to be impulsive, to want everything to happen overnight. It is a time to be patient, to be understanding. If an adult cannot find the resources for patience, then it is wise to seek help from a competent professional counselor.

3. Parents should maintain as stable an environment as possible. Children should continue living in their regular homes, going to their regular schools, playing with their regular friends as much as possible. They have enough to adjust to. Other changes should happen at different times. Of course, this is the ideal, and the ideal is not always possible. What is economically possible most often becomes the norm. One part of creating a stable environment is allowing access to both sets

of grandparents. These relationships are even more vital during the experience of a divorce.

4. Parents should not become defensive and let guilt drive them. It is very normal to feel guilty about a divorce, and this often creates a need to defend. It is so tempting to attack an ex-spouse, but this simply creates more tension for the children. Children know they must keep peace with both parents, and we should be most careful not to place the children in a situation where they are forced to take sides. Children already know what has happened and how much blame to apportion to each parent.

5. If there have been problems of chemical abuse, or physical abuse, parents should give the children as complete a picture of the problem as is possible. It might even be useful to take the children to a professional counselor, one who has expertise in the area of chemical abuse, and let this person explain to the children what has taken place.

Because adults in divorce are wounded people, they cannot always be fair in their judgments. When necessary, it is important to bring in outside resources who might be better spokespersons. All of us as adults usually do our best in taking care of ourselves, defending our own actions. Thus, it is often better for someone from the outside to interpret to children what happens in a family where abuse has been a reality.

In summary, we must remember that many feelings are present in both parents and children at a time of divorce. Adults need to give permission to children to express these feelings, to talk about the hurt and pain that is present. It is the most healthy for children to have a parent — ideally two parents — who will listen, who will hear the anger and hurt and not respond in judgment. It takes time. It is a process, and cannot be solved all at once. But patient listening will help our children walk through a divorce to a new future.

## CHAPTER NINE

# Relationships: Old and New

*Talk by Dee Hehir,*
*Starting Over Single Seminar*

MANY OF OUR RELATIONSHIPS CHANGE WHEN we go through separation and divorce, not just the one with our ex-spouse. One which is most likely to be affected is the parent-child relationship. Where not so long before you were one half of a parenting team, now you find yourself all alone at times and playing the roles of both father and mother at other times. Either you have total responsibility, complete with all the daily joys and heartaches (but no spouse to share them with), or you do not have the children at all and feel both the isolation and freedom that comes with living childless. This creates changes in the ways you relate to your children.

Your children's relationships with each other may change also. My children were 14, 13, and 10 when we separated. I was so occupied with holding two jobs and trying to cope with my own loss that my children drew together and began to discuss and share things with each other. That was when the two older ones really began to include their little sister in their conversations.

## RELATIONSHIPS: OLD AND NEW

My first reaction to this was that it wasn't fair. Here I was separated, and now I felt that my children were shutting me out as well. When I thought about it I realized that they were just putting some emotional distance between themselves and the source of their confusion and pain — their parents. I also appreciated what a blessing this was for them to strengthen the bond among themselves. I knew they would have that closeness long after the pain of this divorce was behind them. And they have.

Another relationship loss we suffer is with our friends and neighbors. Sometimes they take sides, perhaps with a partner who stays in the neighborhood. But other times those around us avoid taking sides, or because they don't know what to say or do, they avoid us altogether. Or perhaps they fear the same thing could happen to them. I remember the reaction of one neighbor as she heard about the third neighborhood divorce in less than a year. She gasped, "It's like a cancer!" And so when you are ignored or treated differently, your relationships change.

The extent to which our relationships change depends a lot on what brought us together. If the focus was social and based on activities with other couples, then our relationships may change a lot. But if the focus was a common interest or service, these friendships may not change at all; they may even grow stronger.

Unfortunately, when we divorce we sometimes lose our in-laws too. Legally we lose them as relatives, but sometimes we lose them as friends and companions as well, and this doesn't have to happen. If you want to keep your in-laws as friends, you will probably have to make this clearly known. It is also possible, of course, that to see your in-laws may be just too painful for you at this time, too much of a reminder.

Perhaps you need some time just to be alone, to let go of some of the pain, to adjust. Then maybe you can reestablish these relationships because it's really helpful to you and your children if you can maintain relationships with all of the grandparents.

Sometimes a divorce can be instrumental in strengthening relationships with your own parents. It seems that sometimes parents and adult children have trouble relating to each other as the people they are now. It's as though they have an old snapshot they carry around with them and that's the way they keep seeing each other — the way they used to see them. Something as traumatic as a divorce really brings us into the here and now and makes us relate as the people we are today. It can be turned into a valuable experience.

Thus, it is clear that our relationships change as our needs change. My kids banded together when I began to relate more realistically, and my neighbors and I grew apart as our common interests declined. I found that I needed a new support system made up of some people who had similar experiences, similar hurts, similar challenges, parallel growth.

We need new friends when we become single. Herman Hesse, a German novelist and poet, told us, "Be ready bravely and without remorse to find new light that old ties cannot give." Now this seems like reasonable advice when we are the ones who are changing, but it is a lot tougher to accept when someone else's needs are causing changes in our relationships. Somehow that strikes you as UNFAIR. We don't want things to change. We prefer things the way they were. So we hang on.

It may be very difficult to let go of old relationships. But we can't go on until we let go of the past. We can't make those new single friends until we've let go of our coupled status. But we keep trying to control what is happening to us in order to avoid the changes.

> *As children bring their broken toys*
> *with tears for us to mend,*
> *I brought my broken dreams to God*
> *because he was my friend.*

RELATIONSHIPS: OLD AND NEW

*But then instead of leaving Him
In peace to work alone,
I hung around and tried to help
in ways that were my own.*

*At last I snatched them back and cried,
"How could you be so slow?"
"My child," he said, "What could I do?
You never did let go."*

*unknown*

It is hard to let go. We want to work on it, pray it back, or will it back. We try to deny the reality of what is happening to us. Sometimes it takes a long time to let go emotionally of an ex-spouse or of the pain or bitterness we feel. Some people never let go. But most of us reach the point where we are ready to let go of the past, to go on. This isn't just a decision; it is a process. We may need to do it many times. Giving it to God is one way of letting go.

Perhaps your relationship to God has changed during your divorce. Maybe you began to pray more — or less. Maybe your church attendance has changed. For me, there was a significant change in this relationship. My crisis brought me closer to God, and the year my divorce was final was the year I joined a church. This was not a happy ending so much as it was a new beginning.

One more relationship that may change when going through divorce is the one with yourself. You may not feel very lovable during or after divorce. Your self-esteem may be low. You may need to reestablish your identity when you become single again. I remember thinking that somewhere during my marriage I had lost myself. I remember thinking, "Whatever happened to the neat person I was at 18? How could I lose ME?"

So one of the things I began to do as a single was to

find myself again. It was very interesting and kind of fun rediscovering what I was all about. In finding "me" again, I had to define who I was. What were my opinions, my values, my goals, my beliefs? I even had to discover my various tastes and preferences. I remember looking through the house and asking the question, "Did I buy that couch or that lamp because I like it or because he did?" I really didn't know. It was hard to separate the "me" from the "we".

I started paying attention to the things I really liked and discovered there were so many that I wrote them down — Mozart, snow, babies, autumn, Christmas, chocolate. My list went on to a second page. Then I listed what I didn't like — drunkenness, b.o., opera, Clint Eastwood movies. It was interesting to see how much longer my "like" list was than my list of "dislikes". It was fun to begin to define ME in this way. It felt very good to find the real me again. Then I set out to improve on that me. That felt good also.

We need to learn how to depend on ourselves, maybe even to like ourselves again. Sometimes it's hard to believe that being yourself is enough if you're suffering from low self-esteem. Taking charge of your life is a tough job when you don't feel you can handle it. So rediscover yourself. Observe your reactions, your feelings, your ideas and preferences. Don't judge them, just observe them and accept them. The better you get to know yourself, the better you will like yourself. The better you like yourself, the better others will like you.

You must love yourself before others will love you. If you do not think you are worth it, how will anyone else believe it? You will find that you can be quite happy just being yourself and developing your own potential.

You begin this whole process by asking "why?" "Why do I have to go through this?" "What went wrong?" You spend a lot of time and energy with yourself and your struggles. I came to the point where I was tired of thinking about it. It was time for something new. So I decided to correct my tunnel vision and to venture out.

A friend invited me to a singles group at my church. I was scared, but it turned out to be very good for me. I discovered that I was not unique or alone. There were many others who had been through what I'd been through and they were surviving. They didn't want to sit around and talk about it either. They were busy planning Greek dinners and spring dances and getting on with their lives. They were learning to enjoy being single. And that's just what I did. I learned to enjoy being single — some days in spite of myself.

In the process I made a lot of new friends, some better than I'd had before. I also made male friends for the first time. What a revelation that was for me! Some kids grow up with opposite-sex friends, but I hadn't. So I had (and probably still have) a lot to learn about being friends with men.

The tricky part is what to do about the attraction. Maybe one of you is more than casually interested or attracted to the other. This needs to be dealt with up front if it's a problem for one of you. When I first met one of my best male friends, I knew he was going to be special. Because the only relationships I'd ever had with men were dating, I anticipated a romantic involvement, but it didn't happen. We got to know each other and did many things together or with others in groups, but nothing romantic happened.

I really cared about him and I could tell he cared about me, so I was really confused. I had never had love without romance before. So we talked about it. In the long run, it has been a very special relationship. We can share our highs and lows, give each other hugs and support, and have wonderful talks. Another plus is that our friendship has lasted a lot longer than many of the romances I see.

Another discovery about opposite-sex friendships is what we can learn from them. Men and women are used to relating differently. Women like to share their feelings and discuss their relationships, while men usually talk about doing things. What my friends and I are discovering is that men who want to discuss their feelings often feel more comfortable talking to a woman. Women have always done this kind of sharing, so now men who have a need to open up and share are making friends with women. We are all benefiting by understanding each other better.

It is also very helpful in opposite-sex friendships to see how they open our minds and lives to a whole spectrum of people with a variety of interests to share with us. I think that often in the initial stages of dating we're frequently attracted only to people who meet the prerequisites we've set in terms of personality or looks. One woman I know said that when she was less secure, she wanted an attractive, athletic looking guy to date because it made her feel better about herself.

There are men, too, who consistently date only very attractive women who are much younger than themselves. Making friends with the oppostie sex frees us from some of that kind of thinking and behavior. It makes us more open to a collection of friends with a wide range of personalities, talents, interests, occupations, skills, abilities, and appearances. Men and women can enrich each other's lives by sharing their uniqueness.

It's helpful having friends of both sexes when we are starting over single. Sometimes we are not interested in dating for a while, maybe for quite a while. Yet we do not want to do the same things with the same people all the time. It's nice to be able to get a group together to play tennis, to go biking, to attend the theater or whatever we feel is more fun to do in a group.

Once we are feeling better and getting out and having some fun with people again, we may start thinking about dating and relationships other than platonic friendships. But this may re-kindle the whole subject of broken relationships again, and we may not be ready for that risk.

## RELATIONSHIPS: OLD AND NEW

As we think about relationships, I would like to ask a question. If relationships are so important to us, why do so many of them fail? And if we have failed in the past, how can we keep from failing again?

One of the problems is in terms of the roles that we play in a relationship. If we are quite dependent, we may look for an independent partner. We may repeat negative behavior or enter again into an abusive situation. I have a friend who has married two alcoholics. Sometimes we have a lot of unfinished business; we are looking for someone to meet the unfulfilled needs from a previous relationship.

I believe a big problem with relationships is that we often will not accept the changes that take place in our partner or our relationship. We all change and grow, but not at the same rate and often not in the same direction. Change often threatens our security, so we resist it or try to ignore it.

Problems are often caused by unmet expectations. One partner may have entered the relationship expecting the other to act a certain way and now feels misled. Or one partner may end up trying to be someone he or she is not. Expectations are like a trap that we can set for another. When that person does not do what we expect, we are disappointed. We need to be careful about what we expect from another person. We may be sabotaging the relationships, all the while blaming our partner for not meeting our needs.

We must also be careful not to confuse our wants with our needs. I may want to go out on Friday nights, but I don't need to. He may want me to go to hockey games with him, but he doesn't need me to go. If we start thinking of our wants as needs, we are giving them more importance and power than they deserve. The trouble really multiplies, though, when we start expecting our wants and needs to be met.

Our relationships would be a lot steadier if we expected the following:

— that we will both change and grow;
— that we need to compromise;
— that only some of our needs will be met by our partner; and
— that we be open and honest with each other about our needs, wants and expectations.

Before we talk any more about what makes a good relationship, let's look at some of the reasons new relationships fail. Obviously, many of the reasons are the same reasons the old ones fell apart. However, new relationships also have a special set of problems to face. Finding a relationship when you're young and optimistic is a lot different than when you've been married and find yourself suddenly single again, often with many years in between. There are all kinds of new behaviors, circumstances, and fears with which we must deal.

Children often have much impact on any new relationship. We may seek to schedule our dating and social life primarily around the time they are with us, or perhaps when they are not with us. Second marriages sometimes fail because a parent is torn between the needs and wants of the children and the expectations of the new spouse.

Also, there may be many fears in terms of commitment. After divorce there is understandably a fear in many people of intimacy, of getting hurt again (or hurting someone else). Often much additional time is needed to build trust. We may be suffering from insecurity, low self-esteem, or practicing some self-defeating behaviors. New relationships may trigger old "tapes" (that is, we react to a new partner or situation as we would have to the old one). That can be terribly confusing for both of us!

Sometimes people in the early dating stages have lowered their standards; they feel they are not worth much and anyone who is nice to them looks good. Others are too cautious and too critical, and no one can measure up. It takes a while to sort out all of this and find where we fit. It is so easy to subconsciously sabotage new relationships if we're not ready for them.

What makes a relationship work? Let's look at a picture that might help bring this into focus. All of its components work together to build "trust." The combination of these qualities moves us along the spiral toward love.

**information for illustration:**
**Love**
**Trust**
**Acceptance, Forgiveness**
**Respect for the other**
**Work, Effort**
**Commitment**
**Communication of: feelings problems, concerns, hopes dreams, pains, fears, highs, joys**
**Understanding, Empathy**
**Meeting needs**

Picture a spiral with "commitment" at the center. The next criteria, the "work-effort", will not be put forth unless it is based on commitment. From work-effort flows "communication". We need two-way communication of our feelings, our problems and concerns, our hopes and dreams, our pains and fears, and our joys and highs. When we do this we give each other information about ourselves and about how our relationship is doing. That's how we create "understanding and empathy" which we need in order to respect the other person. In the same vein it is "acceptance and forgiveness" which contributes greatly to our ability to compromise and "let go" of controls. We must compromise if we are truly to meet each other's needs. Isn't this what "love" is all about?

In good relationships the partners are responsible, or more accurately, "response-able". This has the double meaning of being responsible for (or owning) their own happiness and being able to respond to the other person. This requires a balance. We need to spend enough time together to nurture our common interests and goals and still have enough time alone to care for ourselves while maintaining our integrity.

The spiral above is not all-inclusive. There are other extremely important ingredients which could be included. For example, it could include a "sense of humor" or "having fun together". Nevertheless, it is a starting point for us to examine our own relationship, to decide if we are on the right track.

I would like to share with you a theory of relationships that I have been developing over the past several years, with which I have had some fun.

## STAGE ONE

The first stage, of course, is falling in love. It's marvelous. You feel wonderful, you take on a special glow, and everything in your life seems to go well. Your new partner is wonderful also. He or she is everything your "ex" was not and is everything you were looking for. You love to be together, and when you are apart you are thinking about each other, planning romantic evenings and buying cute little cards as gifts. Do you have the picture? Great, isn't it? Unfortunately, stage one doesn't last very long. It is not real; it is a trick to make us forget our fears, let down our guard, and make us want to trust and try again. Stage one lures us in; it's the bait. But if our love is not real, then stage two will cure us!

## STAGE TWO

In this second stage we discover some of the problem areas and begin to worry about them. We wonder if it is worth the effort. We may deal with these directly or sweep them under the rug, only to have them resurface later like Christmas tree needles demanding to be acknowledged. If you are wondering if you are in stage two, you might ask yourself some questions:

Are you feeling that a relationship is an awful lot of work (especially if it might not last)? Do you feel that you are going to have to make too many compromises? Are you wishing — hoping — asking — expecting that your partner make some changes for your sake and for the sake of your relationship? Are you wondering why you got yourself into this again? Are you mentally noting all of your partner's shortcomings? Are you comparing your partner to your "ex" and noting mostly the negatives (my "ex" never....and you don't either)? What happened to stage one when you compared your partner to everyone else, when this person was just wonderful?

It seems like stage two calls our bluff. How serious are we anyway? Are we really in love and ready for a serious commitment, or are we just in love with love? Stage two doesn't pull any punches; it pulls out all of the stops. This is the stage where we discover that our prince or princess is really just another person with the most annoying way of not noticing that he or she is annoying us.

All of a sudden our expectations are not being met. Our needs are not the other's priority. We become very frustrated. Now what do we do? We have probably already mentioned our love and now we are wondering if this is even a good idea.

It is at this point — stage two — that many second-time singles bail out of relationships. Unfortunately, it is probably our state of mind and not the relationship which lets us down. It takes a belief in love and a lot of work for two people to survive stage two.

We have all been in stage one love. Some of these relationships have naively stumbled into stage two. Hopefully, stage three will be entered into slowly, thoughtfully, and deliberately.

## Stage Three

Stage three is commitment. It is commitment to each other and a commitment to working on problems and solving them. It is a commitment to compromise, to listen, to change. In essence, it is an ultimate commitment to this relationship.

I guess I am looking for stage three love someday. Maybe most of us are. But I think that until we are ready, we'll continue to sabotage our relationships in stage two or even stage one.

I want to make an important point here. There is nothing wrong with relationships that do not reach stage three. I think that we often discount stage one and two relationships as the ones that did not work because they didn't last. Short term relationships are also important. We can learn much from them, and they can be a great deal of fun. Those are two good reasons we should not avoid them. I believe they all work, if we learn whatever lessons they have to teach us.

A friend of mine and I had a theory for awhile; each new relationship was better than the previous one. That is how we would rationalize and console each other at the end of our latest romance. And sure enough, the next one would come along and seem better. However, with a little more scrutiny, we found our theory had some gaping holes in it. First, there is no way to accurately or objectively compare one relationship with another. Second, one person may have been great fun while another was very kind and there is no way to compare. I concluded at that point that if the current relationship has in any way improved over the last one, it is because I have grown and learned from the last one and from all of my relationships. I could not be where I am today if it were not for yesterday, so I am grateful for yesterday. This is especially true if yesterday was painful, for from pain comes growth.

All of our relationships, whether long term or short term, can help us to grow in love. In all of the things I have been discussing, the undercurrent has been love. We all think of love differently. To some, love is the romantic love that I described in stage one. Is that love? Perhaps. It certainly is a wonderful feeling, except when we can't sleep at night. But love is much more than a feeling.

It is a state of mind, a way of living, an attitude of acceptance, trust, hope. *Love Is Letting Go of Fear*, by Gerald Jampolsky, is one of my favorite books. The Bible says, "Perfect love casts out fear" (I John 4:18).

Jesus commands us to love: "Love one another as I have loved you" (John 15:12). When we decide to live by this commandment, we make a commitment. A comitment can be a vow of marriage, a pledge of faithfulness, or the simple but profound realization, "This is it!"

When we are recovering from a divorce or the loss of an important relationship, love can aid in our healing. Love is just the antidote for the poison we may be experiencing while grieving. We can't look for love; we need to love someone else or something else. Then we will heal.

Love is also a gift. When we give our love away, we never run out. The more we give, the more we receive. Ideally, I give my love because I am lucky enough to have it to give. And again, ideally, I give my love not because I am looking for anything in return. Giving is its own reward. Love should be unconditional with no strings attached. If any of you have tried to practice that, you know how hard it is. Someone said, "This is why God gave us teenagers, to teach us about unconditional love."

I believe that God put us here to love each other and gave us many different kinds of relationships with which to learn and grow. All of our relationships can help us to grow in love. I wish you love to hold.

CHAPTER TEN

# *T*WELVE STEPS FOR SPIRITUAL GROWTH AND RENEWAL

*Talk by Dr. Vernon Bittner,*
*Starting Over Single Seminar*

WHEN I FIRST BECAME AWARE of the Twelve Steps as they are used in Alcoholics Anonymous, I thought that they would be very good for others, but that I, as an intelligent person, did not need twelve steps to follow for my own wholeness. Well, I was wrong. I have discovered through the years that the twelve steps hold basic concepts of the Christian faith, and it is for this reason that I have reinterpreted them in the light of the Christian faith. For in these steps I see a very valuable structure for my own spiritual growth and healing. Let me explain.

First, I would like to point out that the "Twelve Steps for Christian Living" which I've developed are divided into three major areas: Steps 1-2-3 and 11 deal with our relationship to God. Steps 4-5-6-7 and 10 have to do with my relationship to myself, and Steps 8-9 and 12 center on my relationship to others. What is different about the approach I am taking is that I have attempted to "Christianize" these steps. By relating the steps to Christ, the tone is positive. They are also written in the present tense, for it is only today that I can change.

## TWELVE STEPS FOR SPIRITUAL GROWTH AND RENEWAL

This is important for us to remember as we think about divorce. It is only right now that is relevant; I can't do anything about the past. And it is important that we not stay the way we are, for the best is yet to come. Thus I would encourage you to use the step system on a daily basis, taking one of the twelve steps each day and applying it to your present situation. Say the steps out loud.

The Twelve Steps are as follows:

**1. We admit our need for God's gift of salvation, that we are powerless over certain areas of our lives and that our lives at times are sinful and unmanageable.**

Each of us has some area that we do not manage well. Admitting that we have not "arrived" is important for spiritual growth. Growing emotionally and spiritually is a lifelong process. It is not completed at the age of 21 or 35 or at any other time.

Growth is both exciting and frightening. Discovering in what area of life I am out of control can be disconcerting. For some it is fear — fear of tomorrow, fear of others, and even fear of themselves. For others it is work. We become "workaholics" because we cannot control this area of life. For others it is food. Life is just one series of diets and rapid weight gains for some people. Every one of us has some way in which we medicate our pain, and many times it is destructive. So I need to recognize areas of my life which I do not manage but which manage me. These aspects of my life need to be changed. To be out of control is to be human. To desire healing is to be humane to ourselves and to others.

**2. We come to believe through the Holy Spirit that a power who came in the person of Jesus Christ and who is greater than ourselves can transform our weaknesses into strengths.**

I believe that Christ can transform us. The Apostle Paul

asked three times in I Corinthians 12 that his thorn in the flesh be removed, but it was not. Yet he found strength in his weakness. It is only when we admit to our weaknesses that we can be strong. I used to think that if I admitted in what ways I was weak, then I would really be weak, but strength comes through an honest acceptance of my weakness.

I also have come to realize that what so often happens is that the Lord transforms my weaknesses into strengths — in fact, sometimes they become my greatest strengths. The divorced experience is seen by so many as an indication of a weakness and/or failure. Yet, it has become for many the opportunity for growth. A time of divorce, instead of just being a time of weakness, can be a time for some of the most significant and growth-fulfilled experiences of life. Actually, many who go through a divorce may discover who they are for the very first time.

As a result of going through a divorce, the formerly married person has something very special to offer other people. Anyone who has gone through this pain will never be the same again, and it is not possible for this person to truly understand and care for others in similar situations. What was a weakness can now be one of our greatest strengths. God can transform our weaknesses into marvelous strengths.

**3. We make a decision to turn our will and our life over to the care of Christ as we understand Him, hoping to understand Him more fully.**

In Step 1 we have said, "I can't." In Step 2 we are saying, "Christ can." And now in Step 3 we are saying, "I will let Him." Turning my life and will over to the care of Christ is one of the most difficult things I have to do. I give it to God, and then in the next moment I might take it back again. It is a constant battle.

There is a specific need for us to let go and let God. Someone has said, "Don't pray for anything you are not ready

TWELVE STEPS FOR SPIRITUAL GROWTH AND RENEWAL

to receive." It is terribly frustrating to pray for open doors if we are not ready to walk through that door. We often get stuck in the status quo. We like our security. We do not want to change. However, there will be no healing or spiritual renewal unless we are willing to turn our lives and our will over to Christ.

**4. We make a searching and fearless moral inventory of ourselves — both our strengths and our weaknesses.**

It is most important that we look at ourselves honestly and become aware of both our strengths and weaknesses. Unless we know ourselves, we cannot work on change. To discover who you really are is a most exciting experience, and sometimes more frightening than we would wish. However, if we sense the power of God's love, we will have the assurance that whatever we find will not cause Him to stop loving us.

In Philippians 2, Paul talks about our need to "work out our own salvation." This does not mean that we can save ourselves; it means, however, that we need to be about our own healing, physically, emotionally and spiritually. In order to do that we need to become aware of areas of our lives that need healing, and then work on them with the Lord's help.

So often it is easy to be aware only of our weaknesses. If we would be asked to list both weaknesses and strengths, chances are that the list of weaknesses would go far beyond the strengths. But it is most important to be aware of our strengths, too. God has given each of us magnificent gifts, and in order to use them we must know what they are. There is nothing more rewarding than to discover some strengths that we did not know we had and to see them develop more fully.

**5. We admit to Christ, to ourselves, and to another human being the exact nature of our sins.**

We call this confession. After doing an inventory of our strengths and weaknesses, we become aware of areas in our lives that need to be discussed with another person, someone we can trust. In the Catechism, Martin Luther asks, "What sins should I confess?" His answer is, "...The ones that bother me." It is the problem that bothers me that I need to share with someone else.

Each of us needs someone we can trust, in whom we can confide and talk honestly. Pastors and counselors have discovered that if they do not have a counselor to whom they can talk, they cannot be a good counselor to others. It is often not enough to just confess weaknesses and strengths to God and to ourselves. At times we need to confess them to someone else. Through confession we are able to more fully experience forgiveness and absolution. The forgiveness we have heard so much about now becomes graphically real in the forgiveness given by another person.

It is tragic to see so many who have not experienced forgiveness, who have never confessed to another person the sin or sins that are truly bothering them. There is much therapeutic value in confessing our faults to another person. The assurance that we are forgiven in the name of Jesus Christ by another human being who knows all about us and who can still love us and forgive us is a powerful healing experience. This is a key step in our own spiritual growth and renewal. As James writes in the New Testament, "Confess your sins to one another that you may be healed."

**6. We become entirely ready to have Christ remove all of these defects of character that prevent us from having a more spiritual life style.**

Working this step is very difficult. To become entirely ready to have Christ help us to remove our destructive life styles requires a strong commitment on our part. In fact, to change destructive life styles requires that we are truly committed to this change. Changing has to become one of the most important things in life. Otherwise, it won't happen. Bad habits die hard. As someone once said, "Destructive behavior is like a living organism. It dies hard."

Destructive behavior is also difficult to change because we get something out of almost everything we do, even if it is destructive in nature. There is a payoff for everything we do, even if it is sinful behavior. Otherwise we would not do it. Therefore, destructive behavior is hard to change.

For instance, let's say that a man has a very bad temper. You might wonder how a person could get any kind of rewards out of a bad temper. But the obvious payoff for this is that people will usually do what this person wants them to do. If they do not accede to his wishes, he will probably explode all over them. So the payoff is that this person gets what he wants, and if it works, why change it?

Becoming entirely ready to remove my shortcomings is difficult, and change will only happen if we are truly committed to making it happen.

### 7. We humbly ask Christ to remove all of our shortcomings.

Changing destructive behavior requires humility, and humility for many of us comes when we have no other choice but to change because the pain with which we are living motivates us to change.

Let us call her Mary. Mary came to the hospital every spring with depression. After her last discharge, she was referred to me for counseling. In the first session I asked her the question, "For whom are you getting sick?" Her response was, "My husband, he makes me sick." "What do you want to do about it?" I asked her. "Well," she said, "I can't get a divorce because it is against my religion. Besides, my brother got a divorce a couple of years ago and my mother almost had a stroke. I can't do this to her." Even though getting sick is not a very appropriate way to deal with a marriage problem, living with the guilt of divorce did not seem to be a very viable solution for her. However, a short time later her mother died, and two weeks following this death Mary filed for divorce.

Divorce is never God's intention, but sometimes it is the only solution, especially when one or both people are unwilling to work on their marriage. My desire is always to help people help themselves so they can work out their marriage to become a creative and growth-producing experience. But I know that I cannot help save anyone's marriage unless both partners wish to work on themselves as individuals, and then on their relationship with each other.

I usually say to the people I counsel that the most important thing you can do is to work on yourself. The only person you can change is yourself. You cannot change your spouse, only yourself. You can leave the marriage, that is true, but unless you have changed or have been changed, you will probably do the same thing in another marriage. So often people will unconsciously pick the same kind of spouse in the next marriage, unless they change.

For example, if a person tends to be an enabler, you are most likely to pick another person who wants care. There are so many people in our world who are takers. But none of us needs a taker, we need a giver. We need to change those destructive life styles with Christ's help. This must become the most important thing in our life. "If any one is in Christ, he (or she) is a new creation; the old has passed away, behold, the new has come" (II Cor. 5:17).

**8 and 9. We make a list of all persons we have harmed and become willing to make amends to them all. We make direct amends to such persons whenever possible, except when to do so would injure them or others.**

When I think of making amends, I think of two things: being willing to apologize for the wrongs that we have done, and secondly, being willing to forgive.

The first one is often the most difficult thing we can do

## TWELVE STEPS FOR SPIRITUAL GROWTH AND RENEWAL

because our pride gets in the way. But the second is not far beyond; forgiveness is tough, and many of us carry resentments around for long periods of time.

In my own situation, I was angry at a lot of people in my life. My mother died when I was seven years old, and so I was mad at her for dying. My father deserted us, and so I was also very mad at him. My grandmother came to live with us for a couple of years, but then she died. An aunt came and lived with us for a few more years, and then she died. Finally I ended up in a foster home. I had so many losses so early in my life.

I had the most difficulty in forgiving my father for leaving. In fact, I never forgave him until after he died. I am not proud of that. But when he died I had a very difficult time going through the grief of that death because we had not been reconciled. I also felt a lot of guilt.

However, I have discovered that the reason I did not want to forgive my father was that I was getting a payoff from staying angry at him. I could excuse some of my dumb behavior with the words, "Well, what can you expect from a kid who lost his mother at seven and whose father deserted him? You really can't expect much of me." And so I would excuse a lot of my behavior. In essense, forgiving my father became the equivalent of becoming an adult.

When I decided that I wanted to grow up and take responsibility for my own life, then I forgave my father. I also began to understand that if I had lost my wife as he did, maybe I would have done the same thing. I also might have been irresponsible, and when I began to realize that, it was easier for me to forgive.

The only solution to resolving resentment is forgiveness. I already gave you one definition of forgiveness. Forgiveness is not liking or trusting that someone will change, it is simply letting go of the hurt and anger so you can feel better. If we don't get rid of the anger, it can very possibly affect our health.

Just about everywhere we look today, there is someone who is talking about stress. Bookstores have many books on the subject, seminars are offered in many settings. We are very conscious of how stress impacts each of us. We know that it causes high blood pressure, heart problems, and physical ailments of many kinds. We also know that we must find ways to get rid of stress — talking, exercising, changing our lifestyle.

One of the biggest causes of stress is resentment. Maybe you have read Simonton's book *Getting Well Again*. Simonton is a physician from Texas who has written a book about cancer patients. What he says, in essence, is that people who do not handle their stress properly, who keep the stress bottled up inside, are more likely to get cancer than people who manage stress well. The reason for this is that stress lowers our immune system. We are not able to fight off disease, whether it be the common cold or whether it be something as serious as cancer.

I am sure we know what this means. Often when we are going through a time of stress and are burning the candle at both ends, we get sick. Maybe this is all a part of God's plan. He knew that the only way some of us would relax is if we would get sick.

The next time that you get a cold, ask yourself, "What stresses are going on in my life?" I do not want you to feel guilty if you get sick, because getting sick is a part of being human, but just ask the question, "What is going on in my life? What stresses am I not dealing with?" As we know, the cold germ is in our body all of the time. Whether it causes some kind of illness depends mostly on our resistance.

Resentment can also affect our emotional health. Depression is really anger turned inward. It is not surprising that depression is the most common emotional problem in our society.

Resentment can also affect us spiritually. One of the definitions of sin is separation. I do not believe that there is anything which separates us from God, from our neighbors, or from ourselves as significantly as resentment, as not being reconciled.

Sometimes the most difficult person to which we must make amends is ourself. Maybe we are angry at our spouse, or we are angry at God, or we are angry at that other man or woman; however, the person we have the most difficulty forgiving is ourself. So make sure to forgive yourself, because if you do not you will make more mistakes, just like the ones you have already done.

If you cannot forgive yourself, then go and talk to someone you can trust. Talking to another can be very helpful in our healing. Someone has said, "I don't know what I think, I haven't said it yet." Sometimes the only way I begin to know why I am having difficulty forgiving myself, or why I am having trouble forgiving others, is because I don't know what I am thinking about that particular person. So talk to someone else. Learn to forgive yourself.

**10. We continue to take personal inventory; when we are wrong, we promptly admit it, and when we are right, we thank God for His guidance.**

As we grow in our spiritual life, we are better able to admit when we are wrong, and we are also better able to admit when we are right. I think this is of great importance, to admit when we are right, as well as when we are wrong.

And we need to do this daily, to take personal inventory, to look at our strengths, what we have done which is right and what we have done which is wrong. This will give us the opportunity to capitalize on what is right and change that which has been destructive in our lives.

**11. We seek through prayer and meditation to improve our conscious contact with Christ as we understand Him, praying for knowledge of His will for us and the power to carry out His will.**

One of the most important aspects of personal growth and spiritual growth is our prayer and meditation life. This is often hard to stick to; we are sometimes so eager to reach our goals that we do not want to spend time in the process. And one of the most beautiful processes is prayer and meditation.

Women often have an easier time here, for they tend to be process oriented, while men so often are riveted on goals. This is one thing I am trying to learn in my own life, to take time to smell the roses, to enjoy the process rather than just the achievement of goals.

The Psalmist says it well, "The Lord is my light and my salvation, whom shall I fear, the Lord is the strength of my life, of whom shall I be afraid?" This puts my frustration into a new perspective.

Or the words of Jesus in Matthew 6 where he tells us not to worry, to remember the birds of the air, the flowers of the field, how God takes care of them. If he takes care of such as these, how much more will he take care of us.

Spiritual growth only comes through discipline. This often happens best through prayer and meditation.

**12. Having experienced a new sense of spirituality as a result of these steps, we realize that this is a gift of God's grace. We are willing to share the message of His love and forgiveness with others, and to practice these principles for spiritual living in all of our affairs.**

If we do not share what the Lord has done for us and with us, it is going to wither up and die. Our faith will atrophy. We need to go public with our faith. There seem to be two reasons why this is so difficult.

First, I think it is because some people have not had a spiritual awakening. I can almost guarantee you that if you follow these steps, you will have an awakening, a spiritual renewal of your life. These 12 steps represent the basic concepts of the Christian faith. If we follow them in a disciplined way,

**TWELVE STEPS FOR SPIRITUAL GROWTH AND RENEWAL**

we can experience Christ in a new way.

Earlier I mentioned that some people have never experienced the forgiveness of God because they have never done a fifth step. I also think there are some people who haven't experienced God's grace — His forgiveness, peace and serenity — because they haven't been working on steps six and seven. They have not changed destructive lifestyles and continue to do the same things all over again.

It is clear, of course, that we will never get to the point where we are perfect, but we need to keep working on our growth. If we have not worked steps eight and nine, if we haven't made amends with some important people in our life: a parent, an ex-spouse, a child, a sibling, a friend, then how can we possibly feel as good as we should about our life? We can't. We cannot really experience God's serenity, peace, and the abundant life unless we do some of these steps.

A second reason why people do not witness to their faith is that they do not know how to do this. There is no "how" in just sharing your own spiritual journey, whatever that may be. When you share with another your strengths and weaknesses, your victories, your failures, it is just a matter of doing it. The only way to learn to do it is to do it. Look for some kind of a small group where you can share your journey. Hopefully, the church is becoming a place where you can talk about your strengths and weaknesses, where you can feel safe in sharing your own life and faith.

I commend to you these twelve steps. It is my hope and prayer that these steps can be instrumental in your recovery process.

# CHAPTER ELEVEN

# STARTING OVER SINGLE

IT IS TIME TO START OVER SINGLE. The shocking and oftentimes unbearable truth has truly set in; you know the marriage is over. No amount of working, hoping, praying, or giving can put it all back together again. The court appearances have ended, the new living arrangements are in place, and the initial grief experiences are behind you. It is time now to come out on the other side. It is time to start over.

There is a strong temptation to want to hang on to the past, to hold fast for as long as you are able, to not want to let go. It is especially tempting to hang on to the resentments, to live in the dreams, to be immersed in the pain. We have an enormous resistance to finally saying goodbye. But the time has now come to do that, to move on to a life after marriage.

Above all, we need to remember that God is on the side of life. God is on the side of starting over, of forgiveness, of release from pain and judgment and self doubt and despair. God gives us the freedom and the courage to start over again. In Christ, the old has passed away, and the new has come (II Cor. 5:17). Divorce is not the end of life. God is on the side of healing, and continues to pour new life into our tired beings.

## STARTING OVER SINGLE

Hopelessness is changed into hope.

Starting over single means that the long winter of suffering and pain and heartache is over, and that the new life of spring has arrived. New life is breaking out all over. As the ice melts we can begin to smell the new fragrance and aroma of spring, and to see all of the freshness and greenness and beauty of the world. This does not mean that winter will not return, but it means that spring is now upon us in all of its splendor. God has brought a new dawn to us in the midst of the darkness.

To start over again is sometimes frightening, sometimes exhilarating. Someone has said that the reason the game of golf is so popular is that it gives us eighteen chances to start over again. We take seriously the words of Revelation 3:8: "Behold, I have set before you an open door, which no one is able to shut." The door to the future has swung wide open. God has given us a new chance to start over.

Lloyd Ogilvie in his book, *Life Without Limits*, gives us a very graphic picture of starting over as he discusses Mark 6:7-13. Jesus, in the verses here, has sent out the twelve disciples to preach and to heal. He knows that the response to their proclamations will not always be favorable, so he gives them some instruction on how to respond when they are rejected. In verse 11, "If any place will not receive you and they refuse to hear you, when you leave, shake off the dust that is on your feet." Shake the dust off of your feet.

Ogilvie, interestingly enough, calls this the "Sacrament for failure". That is a very good description of what we need. When we have ended up in brokenness and disharmony, when we have experienced pain and rejection, when the future looks dark, then it is time to shake the dust off of our feet. It is time to move on, to begin again. Let the past be gone, and be open to the future that God gives to us.

Christians live as Easter people. Easter means that Good Friday is now past. It means that the suffering and the pain of the past have been overcome by the new life and resurrection of Easter. No matter what the Good Friday might be in our lives, no matter what darkness we may be experiencing, Easter shouts the loud refrain, "Jesus Christ is risen, Alleluia!" Good Friday has been defeated. Easter has come.

The message of Easter rings loud and clear like the call of a bell, "Let Good Friday go." Let it go. Let go of the grief, let go of the sorrow, turn to the light, feel the warmth of the Son. Let Good Friday go. Talk about the grief and the hurt with someone who cares, shed the necessary tears, remember and learn from the past, but then let it go. Good Friday has been rolled away like the stone at the tomb. Let God roll away the many burdens in your lives. Whatever the Good Friday might be in you, let it go.

Let us call her Sandy. Sandy had been married for twelve years when everything fell apart. The marriage had not been smooth sailing for some time before the end, but when it failed she sank into a time of deep despair. She did not want her marriage to end, and she tried everything in her power to keep it going. Nothing could repair the broken relationship.

After a long period of grieving, Sandy decided that God was giving her a new future, that the best was yet to come. She decided to make the best of it, to let go of the past. She dedicated herself to spending more quality time with her children, and that part of her life was enriched and strengthened. She enrolled in some college classes and began to discover many talents and gifts and aspirations which had been hidden. She began to see herself as a person with potential and possibilities.

Sandy always saw herself as being married. That was the dream she had for herself from very early in her life, and even after the divorce, she did not want to let that go. She had somewhere in her mind that it was just a matter of time before she would meet "Mr. Right". Somehow, somewhere, there was this perfect man who would sweep her off her feet and give her the love and happiness she needed.

## STARTING OVER SINGLE

As time went on, as she became more comfortable with her singleness, she made a remarkable discovery. Sandy found that she actually enjoyed being single. It was very surprising to her, for she had believed that the single life would never be complete, never be fulfilling. But now she found that much about single life was not only tolerable but also even enjoyable.

Sandy has not ruled out another marriage, but she is very fulfilled as a single person. She has many wonderful friends, not the same friends she had when she was married, but single friends. She also has plunged into the life of her church, caring for others going through divorce, and sharing in the leadership of that congregation. She has a meaning and a purpose which she did not have when she was married and feels that God has used this Good Friday experience to bring about a new future for her. She still mourns at times for her marriage but feels that her new single life has provided a beautiful time of discovery and richness for her.

She also has learned how important it is at the time of a divorce to truly start over single. Many persons want to start over married right away so they jump almost immediately into a brand new marriage before the first marriage has been grieved for and accepted. Sandy found that it took her more than a year to learn to start over single. Some of her friends who have experienced divorce have taken two years or more. Starting over single has been a time of growth and new life for Sandy, and she is surprised by how she has grown and matured.

Let us call him Jim. Jim was married for eighteen years. These were very difficult years, for he was married to an alcoholic. Three beautiful children were born to this marriage, but as time went on these two boys and a girl became the only ingredients keeping the marriage together. Jim decided in the midst of the pain that he would not leave but would stay in the home and pretend. Virtually all communication had ended with his wife, but he dearly loved the children and did not want to leave. As far as the outside community was concerned, all was relatively normal, but if those on the outside had looked closely, they would have noticed that Jim and his wife were hardly ever seen together.

At the activities of the children, friends usually would see one parent or the other but hardly ever the two of them together. They attended different worship services on Sunday morning, he traveled quite a bit, and she always stayed home. They were living together as strangers. This went on for several years.

Fianlly, the situation became unbearable, so Jim decided to move out. Counseling had not resolved any of the problems, and his wife refused to get help for her drinking. So Jim left. He still was committed to a very close relationship with his children and now spent more time with them than he had while married. One of the children experienced emotional problems through all of the tension and turmoil, so Jim spent a great deal of time and effort in working with this situation. He was so busy dealing with the life as a single parent that dating and remarriage hardly entered his mind.

But one day about three years after his divorce, Jim met Sonja. Something clicked between them. This was a great surprise to Jim, for he had not been looking for a new relationship. He had been spending all of his time at his work and with his children. He did not believe he had the time or the energy for a new partner, but he was taken by surprise. This new relationship quickly grew into a very loving and caring romance. A year or two later Jim and Sonja were married. In many ways Jim was reborn. He was a brand new person. Joy and hope returned to his life. Starting over single for Jim led to starting over married.

God is on the side of starting over whether it is starting over single, or whether this eventually becomes starting over married. Every day is a day of grace. Every day is a gift of a gracious God, and we are given the opportunity to experience rebirth. Let go of the past and grab onto the future. Find a church where Jesus Christ is at the center of the people and where divorced persons are accepted as persons whom Christ loves.

Help that church care about single persons. Initiate ways to help others start over again. Sensitize the pastor and the leaders of the church to the needs of the single persons and help shape the ministry of that congregation. Some years ago some single persons in our parish gave me a copy of the book, *Saturday Night, Sunday Morning,* by Nicholas Christoff, and it had a profound effect on me and on my ministry. Help your congregation truly become a caring community sharing Christ's love with all those who hurt.

The best is yet to come. You have been created in the image of God. You have been given infinite worth. So begin again, start over. Get up out of that bed of pain and self judgment and walk. Remember the words, "I can do all things through Christ who strengthens me" (Philippians 4:13). Let go of the past and go into the future with confidence and courage. And always be assured that God will go with you every step of the way.

# APPENDIX

# How to Make an SOS Course Work

One of the major purposes of this book is to encourage individuals and congregations to look carefully at beginning a Starting Over Single program. It certainly does not need to be called by this name, but we would hope that many churches would take seriously such a ministry for those who have been divorced. The need is very great, and it appears that the crisis of divorce will not end soon.

There are three things needed for a local congregation to provide such a program:

1. There should be an openness of the pastor or pastors and the congregation to those persons who have gone through the pain and agony of a divorce. If our small part of the body of Christ welcomes divorced persons with open arms, with love and understanding, we will be surprised by how many singles will want to be a part of our ministry.

2. There should be some divorced persons from within the congregation who can give active leadership in this area. It is always possible that a pastor or other interested leader could plan and implement such a program, but it is more effective and has more credibility if it involves people who have been there.

3. There need to be sufficient numbers of divorced persons living in proximity to the church for such an outreach to

APPENDIX

find a response. This will not be a problem in most urban areas as there are often more single persons than married. But it may be that some smaller communities will not have a large enough base from which to draw.

There are always some specific steps to follow when a new program is planned. Some of these are based on common sense, and anyone who has planned programs before will know and understand these dynamics. Yet, it took us several months to do the planning, and after our first attempt we changed a number of decisions that we had made. It perhaps will be helpful for us to share our experience and make specific recommendations on particular details of the seminar.

Some of the steps that need to be considered include:

### 1. CREATING A TASK FORCE.

The first action to be taken involves the establishment of a task force. This group should include members of the congregation who have been divorced and would like to help others who are going through such an experience. It should also include a member of the church staff. It is important that the task force involve some representation from the decision making body in the congregation so that when plans are made, they can be implemented. No one wants to spend a lot of time and effort in planning and research and then see these plans vetoed by a legislative body in the congregation.

By way of example, Prince of Peace created a task force of five persons. It was made up of the senior pastor and four persons who had been divorced and were now single. The church council was informed of this group and kept appraised of its progress. Thus, there was no problem moving ahead. It took many meetings to put all of the ingredients together, but with the help of this appendix, it should not take other congregations as long.

## 2. Defining the Purpose.

It would be possible to have many different purposes for such a program. At Prince of Peace we determined that our goal was to provide help and support for those who were going through the pain of divorce, and for those who had been divorced. There was no intention to try to recruit new members for the congregation, although that certainly became one of the effects of this ministry. We also were not intending to find some new source of revenue to fund other programs in the church. It was not even clear at the outset that this would be self-supporting.

Above all, our purpose was to be supportive, understanding, and compassionate. There was to be no attempt to lay some kind of guilt trip on these hurting people or to try to convice them to return to their ex-spouse. We took the death of their marriage seriously. We wanted to accept them right where they were, and to bring Christ's message of love and forgiveness and hope. We were not out to convert anyone or to clobber them with the law. We only wanted to respond in love with the Gospel.

## 3. Selecting the Target Area.

From the beginning we were determined to invite anyone in the wider community who had been divorced. We did not want to limit this ministry to people in our congregation, or to those from our particular denomination, or even to Christians. It was clear to us right away in the first session that large numbers of people going through divorce stay away from church. It is the last place they feel comfortable and welcome. So our efforts were directed at providing a welcome and a growth experience for anyone who wished to come, regardless of background, and we especially concentrated our efforts on those who were outside of the congregation.

There was a great deal of discussion in our task force about whether this ministry should be for all people who were starting over single. Should these seminars be for those who have been widowed as well as those who have been divorced? We concluded that it was not wise to mix these two groups because there is so much that is different about the death of a spouse and the death of a marriage. We felt that it would be preferable to have two different programs and two different kinds of support groups rather than trying to combine them into one.

**4. PUBLICIZING THE EVENT.**

Because our intention was to invite people from the wider community, it became very important that we find ways to communicate this information. Each community has different resources for communication. It is best to use as many of these as possible. We placed notices in each of the newspapers that serve our area, and these were possible with no cost to us. We also purchased low cost radio announcements, but found that we relied mostly on free public service radio. With cable TV coming into our community, we are now also utilizing this medium for publicizing such an event.

We printed thousands of brochures and gave them wide distribution. We intentionally communicated with the singles groups in our area. We talked with those at other churches as well as those which were not a part of any church. We found other congregations very helpful in distributing this publicity. We also asked the singles group at our church to help sponsor the first seminar. This had the effect of giving them ownership as well as encouraging many of them to attend. It is essential that people know about this program if they are to attend.

**5. PREPARING A BROCHURE.**

Nothing can doom a program more quickly than a sloppy brochure. People often evalutate the worth of a program by the quality of the brochure. In order to make a quality brochure, it will probably cost some money. We decided to have our brochures printed by a local printer in order to have a high quality publicity piece. If you would like a copy of the brochure we use, please write to the address listed at the end of this appendix.

If possible, the brochure should contain a picture and a brief biographical sketch of each person who will be giving a presentation. It should also include a brief statement about the subject for the evening. We placed our brochures in Sunday bulletins as well as mailing them out with church newsletters. We were pleasantly surprised at the number of our members who are not divorced who passed the brochure on to someone they knew who was in that situation. This itself becomes a form of evangelism and outreach.

6. COST TO PARTICIPATE.

A basic principle about human beings seems to be that whatever costs money is more highly valued than that which is given away. If people pay something for the seminar, even if it is very little, they will take it more seriously. At the same time we realized that one of the realities of divorce is often a severe financial crisis, so we did not want to charge very much. Whatever amount is charged is helpful in covering most of the expenses — the costs for outside speakers, brochures and publicity.

While there is a cost, we also emphasize that there are scholarships available for those who just don't have the money. We are always willing to give free registration to anyone who requests it. We do not want to prevent any person from attending because of financial considerations. In addition, persons who have attended the Starting Over Single program are always invited to come back to additional seminars at no cost. We have had many persons come back numerous times. Working through a divorce often takes a long time.

APPENDIX

## 7. REGISTRATION PROCEDURES.

It is best if people register in advance. The brochure contains the proper forms which can be returned to the church office. Others will choose to call in the registration. It is also important to be prepared the first evening, and even subsequent evenings, for people who want to register at the door. Members of the task force should be present at least an hour before the seminar begins to coordinate all such efforts.

It is not easy for many of the participants to show up at such an event, and some of them appear to be almost in a state of panic. For a few it may even be the first time they have "gone public", admitting by their presence that they have joined the ranks of the divorced. Thus, it is most important to see that each person is welcomed — warmly, enthusiastically, diplomatically. Obviously, we are not glad that persons are going through divorce, but we are genuinely pleased that they have ventured forth to join us for the seminar.

Nametags are important. They can be prepared ahead of time for those who have registered, or each person can make his or her own. It is helpful to provide a folder for each participant. This folder can contain a brochure highlighting the content of each evening as well as additional information about any singles groups. Also provided are blank pieces of paper for taking notes. A folder also provides a place to put any materials that might be handed out by the presenter.

## 8. NUMBER OF SESSIONS.

We have five evenings in our program, but there is nothing sacred about that number. We began with four, but then the evaluations strongly suggested that we consider an evening devoted to discussing "children of divorce" so we changed. Five sessions are long enough to give some depth to this area of concern, but are not too long as to become oppressive. We would certainly recommend that it not just be two or three sessions, but also that it not be many more than five.

### 9. Evening of the Week.

Sometimes the problem of scheduling becomes very difficult in the church. There is no perfect time for anything. We found it best to schedule these seminars on Sunday nights. During the week we ran into so many work conflicts, school activities, and so on. Sunday seemed to be the best night for most. Even those who were away on the weekend could return in time.

The major problem with Sunday night did not come from the single people, but rather from other activities at the church. A church building or program may already be filled. However, most participants are not now actively involved in the life of a congregation, so this will not compete with other programs. The conflict often comes with scheduling the leadership rather than with the participants.

### 10. Time of the Year.

We hold two groups of seminars each year. We may expand that in the future, but two seem to be enough at present. We try to hold one of these in the early fall, shortly after children go back to school, but before the heavy holiday season beginning with Thanksgiving. Thus, we begin in the month of October, perhaps a week earlier or a week later if necessary. If Sunday falls on Halloween, we try to avoid that conflict.

Our second series is held shortly after the beginning of the new year. In Minnesota it is best to avoid the cold months of January and February. Therefore, we try to schedule this series for the month of March, completing it before Easter. Once Easter is over and spring is upon us, the scheduling conflicts seem to mount.

### 11. Format of the Evening.

We schedule our seminars from 7 p.m. until 9:30 p.m. This gives us sufficient time to provide both a large group and a small group experience. Our first hour is devoted to the

APPENDIX

presenter for the evening. It is the content time. There is a description of the content later in this appendix.

At approximately 8 p.m. we break for coffee and conversation. It is a good time for informal discussion. After fifteen or twenty minutes we gather into small groups for the next hour. This is an extremely important time, for now each person has an opportunity to share feelings, ideas, and concerns. These small groups may be the high point of the evening, for they become experiences of the heart.

At 9:15 or so we gather back together in a large group. The purpose of this time is to summarize the evening for a minute or two and make any announcements that need to be made. We encourage people to come back the following week and to feel free to invite someone else to come with them. A brief prayer often ends the evening. People are given the opportunity to stay around afterwards and just talk.

## 12. LEADERSHIP OF THE SMALL GROUPS.

It would be hard to overemphasize the importance of the leaders. We have asked persons who have gone through divorce and who have a strong sense of Christian understanding to help us in the leadership of Starting Over Single. We provide two training sessions for each of them, giving them much input in listening skills, in handling the feelings of others, in confidentiality, and in keeping a discussion moving.

We have found it works best to have one male and one female as leaders of each group. This provides a balance and perspective that is needed. It is clearly understood that none of the facilitators is a counselor, but rather that they are there to listen and to give support. These leaders gain a great deal from this kind of leadership and they are the key to an effective program.

## 13. LOGISTICS.

Starting Over Single should be held in a room which is

large enough for maximum participation without being overcrowded. It should have good ventilation and acoustics. There should be space for coffee and refreshments to be arranged without interfering with the seating or speaking area. It is most helpful if the seats are comfortable, preferably something other than hard folding chairs. If people will have trouble hearing, a microphone is in order. Also, the presenter might need a blackboard and an overhead projector.

**14. CONTENT OF THE SESSIONS.**

A. *Session One* is crucial. This evening sets the tone and the spirit of the entire program. If the pastor of the congregation can give this talk in a supportive and loving way, this will set a climate of compassion and love. We have centered our discussion for this first evening on the nature of God, on marriage and divorce, and on the role of the church. Much of the content is contained elsewhere in this book.

We try to spend more than a little time talking about how Jesus responded to people who were hurt — the woman caught in adultery or the prodigal son. We also have picked up on the parable of the Good Samaritan, suggesting that the church is meant to be an inn, that place where we should bring battered and bruised and hurt people in our world. We talk about hope and about starting over and hold up a banner which says, "The best is yet to come". It should be a positive, supportive, and encouraging evening.

B. *Session Two* might feature someone who has gone through a divorce and has found some positive and effective ways of starting over. It is not essential that each speaker in these seminars has been divorced, but we suggest that at least some of them have gone through such an experience. In our evaluations we found that those who come often identify most closely with people who have similar stories. This also gives much more credibility to the whole series.

We are fortunate in our community to have a woman

## APPENDIX

pastor at a neighboring church who has experienced divorce, who has both started over single and now started over married. She gives to our group a marvelous perspective about her own journey, and this story is contained in chapter seven of this book. It is always best if a person who shares a personal story can incorporate within that story a Christian witness of faith and hope.

C. *Session Three* might be devoted to dealing with grief. Sessions two and three can easily be switched around on the schedule, but it is most important that we spend some time on grief. Because divorce is a time of death, there is usually much unresolved grief in the participants. It doesn't seem to matter if a person has been divorced for two weeks or ten years, the grieving process is still at work in many who come. We wish to assist them in walking through and eventually beyond some of this grief.

In searching for resources, we have discovered that hospital chaplains are often a marvelous gift to a community and to a seminar. Dealing with loss and grief on a regular basis has given them a special sensitivity that can be shared. We want people to find a way to let go, to move ahead, to start over. The twelve steps as outlined in chapter ten are an example of a way to do this.

D. *Session Four* might be devoted to talking about the effects of divorce on children. We were initially worried that many participants who came might not have children and therefore might not be interested in such a subject, but we have found that most people are parents. It is one thing to deal with yourself and your own emotions at a time of divorce; it is quite another to know how to deal with children.

It is best to invite some person who has had extensive experience in counseling families and children. We are most fortunate to have a pastor on our staff with just these credentials, and this material is found in chapter eight. We recommend that the presenter have a strong Christian understanding of parenting and the role of children so that this session is consistent with the theme of the entire series.

E. *Session Five* should serve as a time of summary and closure, a time for putting everything in perspective and helping people to move on. We discovered that one of the most important questions that now confronts the divorced person has to do with relationships. What about that ex-spouse? What about friendships with the opposite sex? Should a second marriage be considered?

We are fortunate to have a person on our task force who has a very special skill in talking about relationships, in talking about how to start over from a positive perspective. This material is contained in chapter nine. This session is a time to talk about what it means to start over single before one is able to even consider starting over married. People need to talk about what they are going to do in the future, to talk about how they will start over.

## 15. Evaluation.

It is also good to give participants a chance to respond, to give feedback, to tell what has been helpful. Thus, some time should be allowed on the final evening for people to fill out an evaluation form, and a sample is included. We started out by trying to have evaluations each evening, but it was just too much too soon. It is appropriate and desirable in the final session to take five or ten minutes for this.

## 16. Support Groups.

As we have concluded the five evenings, we have found that many people who have attended do not want this fellowship and support to end. Thus, we offer support groups for those who wish to continue. This support consists of five weeks of gathering together beyond the end of the Starting Over Single sessions. We ask some of our leaders to facilitate these support groups, but we rotate them as needed to keep the

APPENDIX

leaders from burning out. We usually have had from one fourth to one half of our participants wishing to continue. The majority of these are persons who have just recently divorced, or those whose pain is the most visible. These meetings are held the five Sunday evenings following the regular program.

**17. VIDEO TAPES.**

Prince of Peace has videotaped the five evening presentations. This means that we can offer video tapes to other congregations as a resource. These tapes can either provide the major presentations, especially where it is difficult to find resource persons, or they can merely be helps in the planning process. They also can be in a church library for those who wish to utilize them.

If you or your congregation are interested in purchasing or renting these tapes, please write to the following address:

Prince of Peace Publishing, Inc.
13801 Fairview Drive
Burnsville, MN 55337

## STARTING OVER SINGLE SUPPORT GROUPS
## EVALUATION

Date _____

1. Which sessions were you able to attend?
   Week I: Church & Divorce              _____
   Week II: Self-esteem                  _____
   Week III: Coping with Change          _____
   Week IV: Family/Parenting             _____
   Week V: Relationships                 _____

2. Which topics were most helpful/interesting?

3. What other topics would you have preferred?

4. Did you prefer the activity-centered discussion or informal discussion?

5. Did the group meet your needs/expectations?
   Comments:

6. How did you feel about your small group size?

7. Please comment on the large group closing.

## EVALUATION

8. Please evaluate your facilitators:

|  | MALE | | | FEMALE | | |
|---|---|---|---|---|---|---|
|  | Very Good | Avg. | Poor | Very Good | Avg. | Poor |
| a) Caring | 3 | 2 | 1 | 3 | 2 | 1 |
| b) Informed | 3 | 2 | 1 | 3 | 2 | 1 |
| c) Good listener | 3 | 2 | 1 | 3 | 2 | 1 |
| d) Helpful | 3 | 2 | 1 | 3 | 2 | 1 |
| e) Enthusiastic | 3 | 2 | 1 | 3 | 2 | 1 |
| f) Too talkative | 3 | 2 | 1 | 3 | 2 | 1 |
| g) Too quiet | 3 | 2 | 1 | 3 | 2 | 1 |
| h) Genuine | 3 | 2 | 1 | 3 | 2 | 1 |
| i) Other _____ | 3 | 2 | 1 | 3 | 2 | 1 |

9. Indicate your age
    20-30 ___   31-40 ___   41-50 ___   Over 50 ___

10. Your stage
    Separated   0-6 mos.___   6-18 mos.___   Over 18 mos.___
    Divorced    0-6 mos.___   6-18 mos.___   Over 18 mos.___
    Widowed     0-6 mos.___   6-18 mos.___   Over 18 mos.___

11. Do you have any suggestions for improving our next sessions?

# BIBLIOGRAPHY

American Lutheran Church. "Teachings and Practice on Marriage, Divorce, and Remarriage." Adopted September 10, 1982.

Arnold, William. *When Your Parents Divorce*. Edited by Wayne Oates. Philadelphia: Westminster Press, 1980.

Augsburger, David W. *Anger and Assertiveness in Pastoral Care*. Philadelphia: Fortress Press, 1979.

Augsburger, David W. *Caring Enough to Forgive, Caring Enough Not to Forgive*. Scottsdale, Pennsylvania: Herald Press, 1981.

Bryce, Gladysann. *Divorce and Spiritual Growth*. Toronto: Anglican Book Centre, 1982.

Chafin, Kenneth. Lecture at Billy Graham School of Evangelism. November, 1980.

Christoff, Nicholas B. *Saturday Night, Sunday Morning, Singles and the Church*. San Francisco: Harper and Row, 1978.

Clinebell, Howard J. and Charlotte H. *The Intimate Marriage*. New York: Harper and Row, 1970.

Correu, Larry M. *Beyond the Broken Marriage*. Philadelphia: Westminster Press, 1982.

Crook, Roger H. *An Open Book to the Christian Divorcee*. Nashville,
   Tennessee: Broadman Press, 1974.

## BIBLIOGRAPHY

Erdahl, Lowell and Carol. *Be Good to Each Other*. New York: Hawthorn Books, Inc., 1976.

Fretheim, Terrance. Lecture at Wartburg School of Theology. Summer, 1981.

Gardner, Richard. *The Boys and Girls Book About Divorce*. New York: Jason Aronson, Inc., 1970.

Gardner, Richard. *The Parents Book About Divorce*. New York: Doubleday and Company, 1977.

Hansen, Philip. *Alcoholism: The Afflicted and the Affected*. Minneapolis: Park Printing Inc., 1980.

Hansen, Philip. *Sick and Tired of Being Sick and Tired*. Lake Mills, Iowa: Graphic Publishing Co., 1971.

Hershey, Terry. *Beginning Again: Life After a Relationship Ends*. Laguana Hills, California: Merit Books, 1984.

Kysar, Robert and Myrna. *The Assundered: Biblical Teachings of Marriage, Divorce and Remarriage*. Atlanta: Knox Publishing, 1978.

Landgraf, John R. *Creative Singlehood and Pastoral Care*. Phildelphia: Fortress Press, 1982.

McRoberts, Darlene. *Second Marriage, the Promise and the Challenge*. Minneapolis: Augsburg Publishing, 1978.

Miller, Keith. *Faith, Intimacy and Risk in the Single Life*. Waco, Texas: Word Inc., 1980.

Miller, William A.*When Going to Pieces Holds You Together*. Minneapolis: Augsburg Publishing, 1976.

Peppler, Alice Stolper. *Single Again: This Time With Children*. Minneapolis: Augsburg Publishing House, 1982.

Petri, Darlene. *The Hurt and Healing of Divorce*. Elgin, Illinois: David C. Cook Publishing Co., 1976.

Rasmussen, Larry. Lecture at Holden Village. Summer, 1983.

Ripple, Paula. *The Pain and the Possibility, Divorce and Separation Among Catholics*. Notre Dame, Indiana: Ave Maria Press, 1978.

Smoke, James. *Growing Through Divorce*. Eugene, Oregon: Harvest House Publishers, 1976.

Smoke, James. *Suddenly Single*. Old Tappan, New Jersey: Fleming H. Revell Co., 1982.

Woititz, Janet G. *Adult Children of Alcoholics*. Hollywood, Florida: Health Communication, Inc., 1983.

Woititz, Janet G. *Marriage on the Rocks: Learning to Live with Yourself and an Alcoholic*. Hollywood, Florida: Health Communication, Inc., 1979.